∞

Rooting Out Hidden Faults

James F. McElhone, C.S.C.

Rooting Out Hidden Faults

What Is the Particular Examen,
and How Does It Conquer Sin?

SOPHIA INSTITUTE PRESS
Manchester, New Hampshire

Nihil obstat: Rev. Felix D. Duffey, C.S.C., Censor Deputatus
Imprimi potest: Rev. Theodore J. Mehling, C.S.C., Provincial Superior
Imprimatur: + Most Rev. John F. Noll, D.D., Bishop of Fort Wayne
March 1, 1952

Sophia Institute Press
Box 5284, Manchester, NH 03108
1-800-888-9344

www.SophiaInstitute.com

Sophia Institute Press® is a registered trademark of Sophia Institute.

paperback ISBN 978-1-64413-648-5

ebook ISBN 978-1-64413-649-2

Library of Congress Control Number: 2021950387

First printing

∞

Contents

∞

Preface

The purpose of this work is to give a practical explanation of the spiritual exercise called Particular Examen. The exercise, as it is ordinarily made, is considered; each type of predominant fault is studied; the effect of each on work, recreation, study, and prayer is shown; remedies are suggested; and the practice of certain virtues is proposed.

The idea emphasized is that character development should be spiritual: a getting rid of faults common to work, recreation, study, and prayer; a growth in virtue through these same daily concerns; a progress toward salvation through holiness.

And should not our work and recreation and study be just as much a part of our spiritual life as our prayers and rule keeping? Should not all things tend to the glory of God, our own perfection, and the salvation of others?

—The author

∞

Rooting Out Hidden Faults

Chapter 1

∞

The Reading of the New Testament

The Particular Examen begins ordinarily with the following prayer:

> O Jesus, living in Mary, come and live in Thy servants,
> by the spirit of Thy holiness, by the fullness of Thy
> power, by the perfection of Thy ways, by the truth
> of Thy virtues, and by the communication of Thy
> mysteries. Triumph over all enemies by Thy Spirit for
> the glory of the Father. Amen.

There follows immediately this short prayer of St. Ephrem:

> O Lord Jesus, open the eyes and ears of my heart, that I
> may understand Thy oracles and perform Thy holy will.

A chapter, or portion of a chapter, in the New Testament is then read: first, to help us to increase in knowledge and love of our Faith; secondly, to help us to know our Lord better and love Him more ardently; thirdly, to help us to serve God more and more faithfully; fourthly, to help us to aid others in a spiritual way.

First, to read the Bible is to grow in knowledge and love of our Faith. The Bible is the Word of God. It is one rule of faith, the other being the infallible teacher—the Church; they are not separated as rules of faith; they are one. Now, it is true that we have been taught what the Bible teaches: in catechism, in sermons, in conferences, through monition and spiritual direction, by counsel in Confession. No one could hope through a sermon or two to receive and understand all that the Church teaches; neither should one expect through one or a few readings of the Bible to receive and understand all that it teaches. The reading of it with prudent guidance should ever be helpful.

Secondly, to read the Bible is to grow in knowledge and love of our Lord, whose life and works the New Testament describes. We follow Him from His birth to His Ascension. All along the way, we listen to what He teaches and we believe. From the very start, we acclaim: "Indeed, Thou art the Son of God!" We believe all that He teaches about right and wrong, sin and virtue, about His mission: His life and works and death and Resurrection and Ascension. Our faith is increased; our knowledge of that faith expands; our love for it develops. The spirit of it falls upon us, as the mantle of Elijah fell on Elisha, and we cannot help loving Him who is responsible for that spirit.

Thirdly, to read the Bible is to be anxious to copy our Lord, our Exemplar, our perfect and divine Model. He who studies Him with eyes of faith is urged to love Him. He who loves Him will feel more impelled to read about Him. The spirit of His presence enters our hearts. We strive to catch something of the goodness that was His. We yearn to think as He thought, to speak as He spoke, to act as He acted. In our human and limited way, we endeavor to practice His perfection.

Fourthly, to read the Bible is to use an efficacious means of developing ourselves so that we may help others in a spiritual way. We are to teach others. In teaching them, we are giving what the Bible teaches as explained by the Church. Consequently, the better we know our Faith, the more we know and love our Lord; the more we strive to copy Him, all the more shall we help others to salvation through goodness.

For such reasons we should read the Bible or listen with strict and humble and docile attention when we hear it read. We should try to acquire its spirit even by memorizing, word for word, the truths it unfolds. Then will the Word of God be in our minds and ever ready for use. Thus we shall think of the glory of God, our own sanctification, and the salvation of our neighbor.

Chapter 2

∞

The Manner of Making the Examen

As to the manner of proceeding in this Examen, the following
five acts, or other similar ones, should be made, corresponding to
the five wounds of Jesus crucified. If the exercise is made alone,
one wound[1] may be kissed at each point.

The five wounds and corresponding acts are as follows:

1. The wound of the right hand: let us return thanks to
   God for His benefits.
2. The wound of the left hand: let us beg of God the
   light necessary to know our faults.
3. The wound of the right foot: let us examine our
   consciences.
4. The wound of the left foot: let us beg pardon for our
   sins.
5. The wound of the heart of Jesus: let us renew our
   morning resolutions.

---

[1]   That is, a wound on a crucifix or an image of the crucified Christ.
    —Ed.

When making each act, we should look at the wound mentioned. The following prayers from the Missal may be helpful in giving the proper spirit of mind and unction of heart:

> O God, who, by the Passion of Thine only begotten Son, and by the blood shed through His five most sacred wounds, hast raised up mankind, lost because of sin; grant, we beseech Thee, that we, who on earth adore the wounds our Savior received, may in Heaven rejoice in the glory that He, at the price of His Precious Blood, hath brought to us.

> O Lord, may we find favor in the sight of Thy Divine Majesty, for we lay before Thee the very price paid for our ransom, the five wounds of Thine only begotten Son.

> We beseech Thee, Lord, that we, who on this day devoutly do honor to the sacred wounds of our Lord Jesus Christ, may henceforth, by the fervor of our life, show forth that we bear those same wounds in our hearts.

Of course, other prayers may be used to obtain the proper spirit of mind and unction of heart. Any memorized prayer, such as the Our Father, the Hail Mary, and so forth, may be used profitably. Nevertheless, we should bear in mind to speak to God in our own way, with our own words. "And it shall come to pass, that before they call, I will hear; as they are yet speaking, I will hear" (Isa. 65:24); "The Lord ... shall say, Here I am" (Isa. 58:9).

Chapter 3

∞

Thanksgiving

Wound of the Right Hand

Let us return thanks to God for His benefits.

> I adore Thee, O my God, and give Thee thanks for
> all Thy benefits, and especially for those Thou hast
> bestowed upon me this day.
>
> As a token of gratitude, I offer Thee the merits of
> Jesus Christ, my Savior, and the Most Precious Blood
> which flowed from His right hand on the Cross.

God is goodness itself. As the sun sends forth rays of heat, as a
flower gives its perfume, as love tends to diffuse itself, so does
the goodness of God go forth from Him to fall as He designs. To
crown His work of creation, God said: "Let us make man to our
image and likeness" (Gen. 1:26). "And God saw all the things
that he had made, and they were very good" (Gen. 1:31).

Having imparted His goodness, God would preserve it and
teach man its value by repeated acts. As a consequence, He chose
a people from whom the Savior would come. To that nation
He gave favor on favor, grace upon grace; mercy crowned all.

Through long years, He was kind to His promised race, though they walked in sin and ingratitude. They had strayed far from Him when He gave Jesus, "the gift of God," for "God so loved the world, as to give His only begotten Son" (John 4:10; 3:16). As Fr. Faber has well said, "Man's imagination can fly far and picture the wildest pictures to itself, dream the most marvelous dreams, and conceive the most improbable combinations; still it could not picture to itself a greater, a more wonderful, a more various, a more perfect love than the goodness of God shown through the Incarnation."

Our Lord went about doing good. His every act drew on His goodness. He was the Good Samaritan and the Good Shepherd; the protector of little children and friend of the poor; the health of the body and the refuge of sinners; who touched and they were healed; who spoke and they were forgiven; "who stooped very low: to the most sin-degraded, the most sin-stained, to those whom sin had trodden in the very mire, but stooped with pity to raise them." How He gave of His goodness! He did not spare; He gave profusely and to all: to the good, to the unworthy, nay more, to the ungrateful and even to the unwilling. He was "emptied of His glory"; "He was offered because it was His own will"; He was redeeming the world. He was redeeming me. "He has loved me and given Himself for me" (see Gal. 2:20).

To read about the goodness of God, to hear about it, to meditate for years upon it, would give only a slight idea of its greatness. God has never done but good, and that in an overwhelming manner. Doing good is His very life. There is not a day, not a moment, in which man does not receive blessings. Every day, God bestows grace on grace, "calling man from evil to good, guarding him from sin, and if he has sinned, cleansing him and aiding him to sin no more." Every day brings a fresh array of

God's favors. Work and study and recreation and prayer tell of the goodness of God, so that if our hearts were silent, the very stones would cry out: "Indeed the Lord is good, and of His goodness there is no end!"

How good God is to each one of us! "Consider the number and greatness of the benefits you have received: your perseverance in your vocation; the means furnished by God to enable you to attain the object of this high vocation; the daily exercises of piety; the frequent attendance of the sacraments; the unceasing vigilance of your superiors[2] and the example of your brethren. Add to all this the interior graces, good motions, and holy inspirations that deter from evil and urge to what is good; preservation from grave faults and from venial sins deliberately committed; the increasing ease that you find in triumphing over the obstacles that present themselves; your ever greater attachment to your vocation; your progress in your studies; your success in your functions and employments; above all, the particular Providence which watches over your bodily wants, your health." Cannot all of us say, "Oh, it is most true that the Lord is good, that His mercy endureth forever!" "O my soul, bless the Lord, and never forget His benefits" (see Ps. 105:1; 102:2 [106:1; 103:1]).

The following prayers may help us to express our gratitude.

Thanksgiving for All Graces

I give Thee thanks, Almighty God, for all Thy benefits, and especially for those Thou hast bestowed upon me this day. Lord, I want to be truly grateful for

---

[2] Meaning religious superiors if you are a religious or, if you are a layperson, a spiritual director or someone else who has legitimate spiritual authority over you.

all the graces Thou hast given me to keep me well, to aid me in my studies, to help me keep the rules, and to be ever faithful to my vocation. Do Thou unceasingly watch over me, so that I may ever be under Thy protection.

O God, of whose mercies there is no number, and of whose goodness the treasure is infinite; we render thanks to Thy most gracious Majesty for the gifts Thou hast bestowed upon us; evermore beseeching Thy clemency that, as Thou grantest the petition of them that seek Thee, Thou never forsake them, but prepare them for the reward to come.

THANKSGIVING FOR SPIRITUAL FAVORS

I thank Thee, Lord, for all the spiritual favors Thou hast given me. I thank Thee for the graces that enable me to overcome the temptations that seek to prevent me from studying as I ought. May Thy grace ever urge me to be faithful to my studies, so that I may persevere in my vocation.

THANKSGIVING FOR TEMPORAL FAVORS

I thank Thee, Lord, for all the temporal favors Thou hast granted me. May Thy grace keep me well, preserve me from harm, and enable me to live my vocation.

Other prayers from one's own heart should be added. Speak to God in your own words; tell Him about your spiritual life, your studies, your recreation—whatever should be said in gratitude to an all-loving Father. Thank Him unceasingly for all the spiritual and temporal favors He has given you. We should learn to appreciate deeply the favors God has granted to us and to our families, our friends, our community. And what better way of expressing our thanks than by the goodness of our lives. "If you love me, keep my commandments" (John 14:15).

Chapter 4

Petition

Wound of the Left Hand

Let us beg of God the light necessary to know our faults.

> O God of my heart, I beseech Thee, through the
> Precious Blood that flowed for us from the wound of the
> left hand of Thy Son, to grant me the grace of knowing,
> detesting, and correcting my faults, that on the Day of
> Judgment, Thy angels may place me, not on the left,
> but on the right hand of the Supreme Judge.

The Holy Ghost is God, the third Person of the Blessed Trinity, proceeding from the Father and the Son from all eternity and equal to them in all things. As we commonly assign the work of creation to the Father and the Redemption to the Son, so we assign the work of sanctification to the Holy Ghost.

The Church is the Mystical Body of Christ. The Holy Ghost is the soul of that Body: directing, guiding, and sanctifying. Through the Holy Ghost the Church, on the first Pentecost Sunday, had her perfect fullness. "It received supernatural and divine powers; it became a true voice, a light, a teacher of the world." She partook of the impress of the Spirit of Truth and Love, who would abide with her forever. The Church "is one, because He is one ... holy, because He is holy; infallible, because He is the light of the truth."

The Holy Ghost dwells in the individual soul. "Know you not, that you are the temple of God, and that the Spirit of God dwelleth in you?" "Or know you not, that your members are the temple of the Holy Ghost, who is in you?" (1 Cor. 3:16; 6:19). He teaches, inspires, and counsels. He brings the grace of the sacraments. He is the sweet comfort of prayer. He is present with sorrow unto penance or joy unto life everlasting. When hope was weak, He imparted His strength; when grace was inactive, He gave it new life; when charity was cold, He poured grace into the soul and all was regenerated. "Keep the good things committed to thy trust by the Holy Ghost" (2 Tim. 1:14).

Would you have wisdom? Ask the Holy Ghost for it. Would you have understanding? Seek it from the Holy Ghost. Pray to the Holy Ghost for counsel, fortitude, knowledge, piety, and fear of the Lord. You can readily see how you would develop if you had those gifts. Have you thought of begging for them? Has your prayer been constant, humble, confidently persevering? If you have asked, you must have received some of the fruits of these gifts: charity, joy, peace, patience, benignity, goodness, mildness, fidelity, modesty, continence, chastity.

We Must Know Our Faults

It is obvious that, unless we know our faults, we cannot detest them and consequently cannot correct them. A study of self very often reveals that self-love has clouded our view, hiding in deceit those faults that are so apparent to those about us and so open to God. No doubt our spiritual director has helped us to see ourselves as we really are; our superior more than likely has come to our assistance; sermons, conferences, and spiritual readings have shed new light on the actual state of our souls. But if such knowledge is to be truly useful as a means of improvement, we should be on the alert not to fall into new faults while we are fighting the old ones.

Prayers for Light

O God, Father, Son, and Holy Ghost, enlighten my mind, that I may know what I have to do or to omit in order that I may procure Thy glory, my own sanctification and the salvation of others.

O my God, from the depths of my misery I dare to raise my voice in supplication to the throne of Thine infinite mercy; may Thy heart, O my God, be open to my prayer! I beseech Thee that I may know myself. Deign to manifest Thyself to me, that I may know myself as Thou knowest me; that I may see all the sins that I have committed and the good that I have left undone.

O Holy Spirit, source of light, dissipate the darkness that blinds me; enlighten my mind that I may know my faults as I shall know them when I shall appear before my Judge to give an account of myself.

O Mary, refuge of sinners, obtain for me the grace to know myself as thy Divine Son knows me. Good St. Joseph, pray for me, that I may know what I ought to do and so earnestly strive in all my actions to do what is right.

Rooting Out Hidden Faults

Reasons for Detesting Our Faults

Our faults, sins, and imperfections offend God. Surely we who are following a supernatural vocation should not be satisfied with the mere keeping from serious or even light sin. We ought to be concerned about those small things of daily life that, if neglected, mean imperfection and very often many imperfections. We would not think of offering serious offense to a friend; nor would we give slight offense continually. How much more anxious should we be not to offend God even in a slight way.

Moreover, our faults keep us from following our vocation as we ought. They hold us back from perfection and the will to strive for it. Mediocrity and carelessness are signs of failure. Spiritually we should want, and desire with a great desire, to be holy. We may not and certainly will not reach the perfection of our Lord, but we can set our hearts on doing our best, and God does not ask for more. To say and to think and to feel sorry for our sins and imperfections — that is, to detest them — is the one way to higher things, is the one means to make our wills strong with earnest effort in the correction of our wrongdoing.

It is surely true that our faults are not the only source of our own unhappiness but are also the frequent cause of the unhappiness of others. Look over your past life; let your conscience bear witness; let your sins testify. Has not sin been the source of worry, remorse, regret, sorrow? For "by what things a man sinneth, by the same also he is tormented" (Wisd. 11:17). Have you not wished that you had not committed a certain wrong? Have you not yearned to begin anew, so that, by avoiding sins, you might retain that peace of mind, that serenity of heart that comes from a good conscience? "The justice of the upright shall make his way prosperous" (Prov. 11:5). Has not your unhappiness affected others? Can you not see that your anger, your uncharitableness, your disobedience, your unkindness, and your harsh criticism have disturbed the peace of those about you? What is more evident than the fact that sin does cause unhappiness?

Prayers for Detestation of Sin

O God, Father, Son, and Holy Ghost, give me the grace to detest my sins as Thou dost detest them. Make me see that my sins and imperfections offend Thee, that they keep me from striving for perfection, that they are the cause of unhappiness to myself and to others. Fill my heart with sorrow for sin, so that I may never sin again.

O Holy Spirit, soften my heart, that I may detest my sins as I will on Judgment Day, which is so terrible even for the innocent soul.

O Mary, Mother of God and my mother, pray for a poor sinner who places all his confidence in thee. St. Joseph, listen to my prayer. All ye saints of Paradise, help me to detest my sins and imperfections.

Correction of Our Faults

When we know and detest our faults, we set about to correct them. We may not, and undoubtedly will not, get rid of all of them at once, but we can be free from all of them through constant and continued perseverance. Now, the Particular Examen is the spiritual means of working against our faults; being a daily exercise, it helps us to determine our progress from day to day. Such improvement, even though it be little by little, must reach to great spiritual success.

Rooting Out Hidden Faults

O God, Father, Son, and Holy Ghost, enlighten my
mind, that I may know what I have to do or to omit
in order to procure Thy glory, my own perfection,
and the salvation of others. Move my will, that I may
efficaciously desire to perform my duties this day.

O my God, Thou dost wish to recall me from my erring
ways, to vanquish my repugnance to Thy holy law,
to rouse me from my indifference, to enlighten my
ignorance, to raise me up after many falls, to give me all
I ask, to help me correct my faults.

O my God, who hast doomed all men to die, but hast
concealed from all the hour of death, grant that I may
pass all my days in the practice of holiness and justice,
and that I may deserve to quit this world in the peace
of a good conscience and in the embrace of Thy love;
through Christ our Lord.

Chapter 5

∞

Examination of Conscience

Wound of the Right Foot

Let us examine our consciences.

> O Lord, how far I have strayed from the path of perfection traced out by the Blood of Jesus Christ! How many faults I have committed this day!

A particular examination of conscience differs from a general examination. The latter embraces all the sins and imperfections committed during a certain period, such as from night prayer to night prayer, or from one confession to another. The particular examination concerns only one subject, and that subject depends on the individual. It covers a short period of time—from one Examen to the next.

∞

The subject of the Particular Examen is one's predominant passion—that is, as it is more commonly called, the predominant fault. A predominant fault is that fault that brings forth one's ordinary temptations or that into which one is prone to fall or into which one has fallen most frequently in the past.

A predominant fault tries to be a master; and "no man can serve two masters," if they are in opposition (Matt. 6:24). Yet there are many who have attempted to follow two masters and give service to both. There are those who have the wrong master. They serve him with diligent devotion. They fix their attention on some special object and seek it with a zeal that will not be denied. That object is very often the acquisition of riches. At the start of such conquest, no doubt there was the idea of being faithful to religious things and hence to God, but as the thought of riches became more and more absorbing, God was more and more lost sight of, and wealth became the master, and almost the sole one. Now there need not be anything wrong in acquiring money. In fact, it is reasonable for those in the world to seek the ordinary comforts of life and to use means that will assure peace of mind for future comforts. But it is decidedly wrong to allow wealth to become too fixed a determination. "What shall it profit a man if he gain the whole world, and suffer the loss of his soul?" (Mark 8:36).

Wealth is a tyrannical master. Honors can also be. Men of the world have been known to fly wealth for honors. Money has not a mastering appeal for some; honors have. Soldiers have foolishly risked death for vain reasons; politicians have thrown away reputations; generals have sacrificed men; statesmen have been malicious liars and stolen the rights of others. Examples could be multiplied to show that men do set their hearts on honors.

For others, the wrong master is liberty, ease, love of pleasure. Liberty is really a tyrant. Some men think what they please; they do what they wish; they are a law unto themselves; they are not subject to higher powers; they sin freely. For others, ease is a master; they are without zeal; they refuse to accept the ordinary responsibilities of everyday life; all things are measured for them by the amount of effort they do not have to put into things. Still others follow pleasure, as a master; there is for them but one thought, and that is—pleasure. How eagerly they seek it; how many sacrifices they make to attain it and walk in its deceiving company; how their hearts are centered in passing enjoyment!

There are cases, and all too many cases, where wealth or honors, ease or pleasure, or all of them have been the master. Yet the more common temptation is divided service of two masters who are in opposition. Such service means trying to work for both of them at the same time and giving undue cult to the wrong one. There are reasonable limits to everything, and it is only when those limits are crossed that fault or sin arises, for going beyond the proper bounds signifies that the Master, who should be served, is being neglected.

Now, have not all of us tried to serve two masters? There are so many small ways that we can give and actually have given divided service. The ordinary affairs of daily life offer many occasions, and we must make a choice. Here is one who resolves to practice recollection. He sees the necessity of it and perhaps even its true value. He begins in the morning with prayers for rising; he continues the day with ejaculatory prayers or thinks of our Lord in the Blessed Sacrament; to some extent, he realizes God's presence everywhere. When night comes, what would an examination of conscience reveal? Would it manifest a day that was given as perfectly as possible to recollection? Would it show a lack of zealous attention and fervor? Would there have been moments of lost opportunity? The service of the true Master should be made an all-absorbing duty.

Rooting Out Hidden Faults

Consider how many try to serve two masters in the way that they practice obedience! They are not rebellious; they simply do not work for the one Master perfectly. Sometimes it is a cheerful obedience that is lacking; at other times, an entire or a prompt obedience; but most often a supernatural surrender of the will is wanting. The ideal would be to have all obey perfectly in all things and in every detail; but we are human and therefore fall occasionally. Still, our motive can be very high; we can try to obey in all things as we would our Lord; we can work for Him personally. The loss of that presence of our Lord, the failure to think that we are doing something for Him, and the lack of realization that we disobey Him when we do wrong mean that we are not carrying our obedience to a spiritual plane that denotes steady and persevering progress.

Could not the true Master be served with a more perfect spirit of mortification? The eyes are prone to be curious and inconstantly wander; they can be given fully to God. The ears are willing to listen to distracting things, to that which pleases the senses, and even to that which means imperfection and sin. The tongue is so ready not to take heed of its ways, and so unready at times, if not frequently, to pray with the fervent attention it should. The mind needs to be brought into subjection. We can be satisfied with imperfect mortification; we can be partially unwilling to strive for better things. We can serve two masters.

Now, what is true of obedience or recollection or mortification can also be true of other virtues. Some hate sin and avoid it; others hate sin and avoid it but not with fullness of purpose. Still others hate imperfection and seek to avoid it altogether; and there are those who hate imperfection yet do not avoid it with a resolute effort. So for meekness, charity, patience, humility—any virtue. Many love God to some extent; they resolve to do all to please Him, to love Him as He should be loved, and then they leave something wanting through their own fault. There are numerous choice souls close to God who need little to make them perfect in the service of the Master.

Ask yourself the question: "Is there any one virtue that I practice perfectly?" Think of the joy of giving the perfect practice of a virtue to God! Think of the intense happiness of living one day in the perfect service of God! Think of the deep satisfaction of living one perfect week for God! Then try to imagine the constant and sweet delight of working perseveringly. Such is the ideal. No one should be unwilling to strive for it, even though the realization never takes place. Perfection may not be reached, but the heart and courage to work for it are not wanting.

Those who seek wealth set their minds on acquiring it with such affection and go after it with such zeal that they forget all else. Those who want honors labor with an effort that is untiring and unbounded. Their service is wrong and woefully wrong, of course, yet they are not to be denied and they surmount all possible obstacles. Such zeal and such effort are more worthy of the true Master. Saul, the Jew, labored for things that required zeal and effort; Paul, the Christian, worked with the same zeal and effort. We can change to higher things with the help of grace.

How good have we been so far? Can we improve? Have we been far from perfection? Not so far? Close? What matters the distance! God is always present with grace. If we have been far from perfect service of the Master, then it will be easy for us to see things to be done. There must be courage. There were three falls on the way to Calvary; our Lord had a purpose in reaching it, and He died there. If we have not been so far from better things, we can still see more to do; our Lord was dying on Calvary for sin, yet He saw our need of a mother, and He gave His Mother to us. He also forgave the Good Thief. Are we close to perfect service to the Master? Then we can understand what St. Francis of Assisi meant when he said: "Now let us begin to love Jesus Christ a little." Though we be rich or poor in a spiritual way, we can try, and try hard, and keep on trying to give our complete service to the one true Master.

As there is no better way of overcoming a predominant fault than by the practice of the virtue opposed to it, each one should seek to learn the detailed ways in which a predominant fault may arise and to learn the various degrees of the opposite virtue. To set one's mind on the avoidance of something wrong, to be resolved to correct it, and to be perseveringly zealous in fighting against it will mean decided success. Nevertheless, far greater fruits will be obtained by the practice of virtue, especially of that virtue opposed to the wrong committed.

Another way to overcome a predominant fault is to practice one's strongest virtue, or, as it is more commonly termed, one's virtue of predilection. Look at the lives of the saints, and you will find that one saint is noted for his humility, another for his poverty, a third for his meekness, a fourth for his intense love of God. The saints did not neglect any virtue; they simply had one that was the central strength of character. Each of us has a virtue of predilection; a little self-study should reveal it; daily practice makes it grow; other virtues have to develop with it.

∞

A further way of overcoming one's predominant fault is fidelity to the practice of the presence of God, which, as St. Francis de Sales says, "is one of the surest means of making progress in the spiritual life."[3] No one practiced the presence of God as perfectly as the Blessed Virgin.

The Blessed Virgin had a vocation. God had determined that vocation, and He prepared her for the dignity and responsibility of it through her Immaculate Conception and fullness of grace. And she, without knowing her vocation until the Angel Gabriel announced it to her, prepared herself. She was practicing virtue perfectly; there was no detail of her daily life that could be more holy. So her progress in virtue was not the advancement of the ordinary soul—a growth from sin to virtue; hers was always a growth in virtue. She was advancing in holiness by making all of her virtues more intense. She was living as perfectly as any creature could possibly live; she was as worthy to be the Mother of God as any creature could possibly be. Grace and her own cooperation were preparing her for her vocation.

The Blessed Virgin, before she knew her vocation, lived perfectly for God. During those years she grew more lovely in goodness. Her virtuous charm undoubtedly exerted a strong influence on others. She had companions who were made better by her presence. She had friends who must have marveled and rejoiced at her fineness of character. In particular, her father and mother gloried in their child of God. Consequently, by the very fact that she was known, she was an influence for good. She did not think of bad example; she did not have to think about it. Perhaps she

---

[3]   St. Francis de Sales, *Introduction to the Devout Life*, pt. 2, chap. 12.

did not think of good example, either, for those who try to live, as she did, in perfection, need not ponder on the responsibility of good example. She was doing for the world that which is so highly spiritual and so deeply charitable—living in such holiness as to draw others to God.

She was also saving and sanctifying souls by a life of contemplation. Her days were spent in prayer. All she did was pray, for she offered all to God and performed all as befits such an intention. Without actually being in religion, she was a religious. She lived in the presence of God; her recollection was habitual; she supernaturalized every detail of her daily life. Trying distractions, created by daily cares, could not gain control over a will made perfect by grace. Spiritual dryness could not make arid a soul burning with supernatural fervor. She lived in perfect prayer. And yet, surely, she did not keep those prayers for herself. She was not spiritually selfish. She prayed for those things dear to the heart of God—the conversion of the world and the salvation of souls. She prayed for that interest close to the hearts of the Jews—the Messiah. She wanted that Promised One to come; she thought it; she yearned for it. It was her prayerful thought.

Then one day, an angel tells her that she will be the Mother of God. Her call has come; her vocation is made known. Her practice of the presence of God is to become a reality. She thinks of that great fact to be; she meditates on the coming of the Messiah; it is her sole thought; how could she think of aught else but the Infinite to be? God's actual presence will make her more intensely perfect; all her virtues will receive a new luster.

A mother's love for her child is without doubt as fine an expression of God's love for His children as we know. The love of the Blessed Mother for her child is the perfect mother love. She watched Him grow, and she grew in love of Him. Perhaps she did not need a Mount Tabor to understand His divinity and to have it always present. Be that as it may, she was close to Him; her home was His tabernacle; for thirty years, she lived in the actual presence of God. She saw God; she loved God; she had the supreme happiness and constant joy of a perfect creature loving God perfectly.

From Cana to Calvary the Blessed Virgin was certainly away from her Son. Not often in the Gospel story is her presence near Him mentioned. Once the crowd told Jesus that His Mother and brethren were present. Yet we know that Christ was in Galilee and the Blessed Virgin must have been there. Undoubtedly she went down to Jerusalem for the prescribed feasts at which He, too, was present. But for the most part, they were separate. Once again, then, her practice of the presence of God is in spirit. Now that recollection must have been centered on the great fact to be accomplished—the Redemption. That was dear to her heart, as to her Son's; and though she saw, as He did, the sorrow of Calvary, she knew also of the glory and joy of the Resurrection. She realized that sin was to have a Victim, and more than ever, she understood the ingratitude, the offense of sin to God. She thought of the humiliation of the Cross, the obedience, the mortification of her Son's death, but she valued all in what was to be done—the world redeemed.

The days from the Resurrection to the Ascension of Christ were certainly days of joy to the Blessed Virgin, and that joy did not cease when her Son ascended into Heaven. In fact, her happiness must have continually increased, for the Blessed Virgin, as no other creature, enjoyed the full fruits of Communion. Hers was the great joy and delicious peace of the Sacrament. Hers was a perfect union with God. And it would not be surprising if those who came under her influence also came under the spell of that hidden presence. Many surely found that the Mother did lead to the Son, that to know the Mother was to know the Son, that to speak to the Mother was akin to speaking to God, that there was an intercession between them, that already the Son was dispensing His gifts through His Mother.

Then once more the presence of God becomes actual to her—she is taken to Heaven to live in the presence of God for others, using her influence for others, interceding for others. We do not know what good the Blessed Virgin did for others in her own day, nor do we dare to imagine the good she has done for others since her Assumption. Think of the millions who are daily invoking her aid; then try to imagine the millions on millions who have invoked her aid in the past. The imagination could run riot and yet would not truly estimate what the Blessed Virgin has done for the world, for God has given her something of His power, and no one can hope to realize the goodness of God.

Would that we followed the Blessed Virgin in practicing recollection! There is no doubt that hers was perfect. We have much to do in making ours perfect, but have we consistently tried to practice the presence of God? We have at our command ejaculatory prayers, acts of faith or any other virtue, spiritual communions or spiritual visits, and meditating on the Blessed Sacrament of God. Furthermore we can live in God's presence by having the proper spirit for our work, or study, or play, or prayers; we can live in the presence of God by making all things prayer, by doing the best we can in everything we do. We can think and speak and act as though we were actually in the very presence of God.

Chapter 6

❧

Pride as a Predominant Fault

The right understanding of things is a necessary step in the way of perfection. The hunger and thirst after justice — after improvement — needs direction; the beginning of wisdom — the yearning and will to be holy — must be orderly; the growth in the knowledge and love of God — the giving of the mind and heart to God — have marks that show the way. To follow these, there must be a thought of spiritual need, a meditation on what has been acquired, a looking backward on the reasons and causes of failure or success, a searching anew for the means to avoid the mistakes of the past, while new courage, fresh resolve, and reborn yearning urge the soul to ascend the mountaintops where perfection waits.

What should be kept in mind in seeking improvement? What are those things that mean betterment? The answer must not be hazy; it should not be general; it has to be particular — something that concerns the daily life, our daily spiritual growth, a habitual effort to make perfect the small actions of each day. The little-by-little fall must have a contrary little-by-little rise. So, each day in the things to be done, there are means of not merely being good but becoming holy, of reaching great heights of holiness.

There are many small actions each day that can be made holy and pleasing to God by purity of intention, by supernaturalizing them, by offering them as clean holocausts to God. Moreover, as these unlimited small actions are kept from imperfection, there arises a growing desire, an intense longing, to work harder and in a holier way: so that orderly satisfaction arises from performing all daily tasks not merely well but perfectly.

When you look at the life of the Blessed Virgin, what is it that strikes you as being her chief perfection? Surely, "He that is mighty hath done great things" (Luke 1:49). She has been preserved immaculate. Her soul has been adorned with grace. She was to be the Mother of God, a morally infinite dignity. She was to stand in a special relation, unequalled and extraordinary, with the Trinity, and she was humble. Mary kept perfect the gifts God gave her; she labored incessantly to return her talents; hers was a liberal and complete offering of self. She made a perfect return to God. See the humble poverty of Bethlehem; reverence the humble obedience of the flight into Egypt; love Mary sorrowing at the foot of the Cross. But Mary, the ideal, the perfect, was nowhere so powerfully manifested as in the hidden life at Nazareth with God. Who shall describe the interior of that Mother all fair, that Mother of grace, in whom was found no stain? Who shall tell of the greatness of her love, the intensity of her prayer, whose life was an interior copy of her Boy? Yet she did not receive the plaudits of that everyday world that looked for the Mother of God in wealth and splendor; she was not distinguished in the eyes of the world for any great, heroic deeds, for no one was looking for heroism in the lesser things of everyday life; still she was leading a life of perfection by making the little acts of daily life the training ground of character. There was a constant effort to strengthen and humble the lesser things of life — things of little importance in themselves yet the very foundation of perfection.

In the little things of daily life, then, two great spiritual forces come into play — avoidance of wrong and increase in virtue. Separately and distinctly, good results may be obtained from these; united, great results must be had. Small actions mean small virtues or small faults or sins. The petty fault, the frivolous fault, the silly fault passes and the humble virtue grows if one be in earnest. The soul may not, and more than likely never will, be wholly free from the slight spiritual stain, but the day soon comes when it advances rapidly and even consciously by the gradual destruction of imperfections and the actual acquirement of certain virtues.

The life of Christ clearly shows the great virtues necessary for holiness. His life was an act of humility — His Father's work must be done — and Bethlehem was its firstfruits: a God born of a humble Virgin in a stable. The hidden life at Nazareth bespeaks humility. Every circumstance of His life in public suggests it. It was the virtue He dearly loved and praised, taught and practiced from Bethlehem to His death on the Cross. "He was emptied of His glory," "humbling Himself" unto death (see Phil. 2:7, 8). "To the Jews indeed a stumbling block, and unto the Gentiles foolishness, but to us, who are called, the power, the wisdom, the glory of God" (see 1 Cor. 1:23–24). The Blessed Virgin and the saints took Him as their great Exemplar and sought to be like Him. The example, therefore, is divine and human; consequently, no mistake can possibly be made by seeking to form the soul with the spiritual character of the virtue thus manifested.

Humility has often been said to be the one virtue necessary for the attaining of others. It is certain no soul is going to reach any degree of holiness without it, for it — the truth about spiritual life and the importance of daily right living—directs all to God and inclines the will to act conformably. God, all; self, nothing: therein is the dependence of the creature acknowledged. God, the Giver of all, to whom all is due; self, the despised servant, who has nothing that has not been received. Hence, all actions are to be referred to God; the soul works for God, not for self, not for the esteem of others. Intention is constantly alive and active in directing that everything be offered for the honor and glory of God. Pride would overrun the true order by making self a predominant master, the god for whom ordinary actions are performed. Pride would have the soul take glory to itself or think of the esteem of creatures; that is why pride is the source of wrong in many ordinary actions—the slight irreverence, the lack of meekness, the willful uncharitableness, the vainglory without number, the distracted, self-centered prayer. On the other hand, if the work of the day is directed by humility, the self-esteem and desire for praise of creatures, so conducive to wrong, will vanish; in their place will come the honest conviction that all is vanity except working for God even to the smallest detail.

Walk humbly before God. Let all things be permeated by humility. Return the given talents to their proper source. Seek to be directed in all things by this all-important virtue. Sanctify, do not mar or destroy, the lesser things. Pray that you may be faithful in offering all to God.

O my God! I want to be humble. Thou art all: I
am nothing. I depend on Thee; without Thee I am
nothing. I have received the gifts of body and soul from
Thee; let me not glory in them as my own, but let me
return them all to Thee for Thy glory. Thou art the
Giver of all that I have and all that I am and all that

I do, and I return all to Thee. O my God, I want to be humble in my ordinary actions each day, that I may please Thee in thus doing Thy will.

Have we not tried to follow two masters in regard to pride? True we are not extremely proud, nor are we perfectly humble. We are proud to a certain degree; we are humble to a limited extent. We are following two masters, giving complete service to neither. The stronger pride is, the weaker is humility. Is pride our predominant fault? Does it bring forth our ordinary temptations? Are we prone to fall into it? Have we fallen into it in the past? "Pride is the beginning of all sin" (Ecclus. 10:15 [Sir. 10:13]).

Pride is an excessive love of self. In thought, or word, or act, it is a neglect of the fact that we depend on God. What we have, physically, mentally, or spiritually, we have received from God. True, we can increase the gifts of God, but even such increase depends on Him. In other words, our talents and the use of them depend on God. Therefore, we should use God's gift for His glory, giving Him credit; we should not take the credit for what we have or what we do.

Pride, then, places one in opposition to God, since it makes one work for one's own glory. Pride is a complete or partial forgetfulness of God. How foolish to work for self! How absurd to serve self! How unreasonable and wrong to forget what we owe to God!

Pride also places a false regard on the opinion of others. We have reason to desire a good reputation and we should seek to preserve it — nay, strive to make it more and more secure. But our motive should not be the good opinion of others. The good opinion of God should be our thought. How do we stand before *Him*? What does *He* think of us? What we do should be for *Him*.

The idea of working for God is especially applicable to those following a vocation. A vocation is a means to serve God better, in fact it is the greatest means to holiness and salvation. Still a vocation is not for self alone. God expects a holier service from those who are called; He demands a striving for perfection. He also commands those following a vocation to help others. That obligation of leading others to holiness and salvation is ever present. Faithfulness to that duty means forgetfulness of self, a true interest in those about us, a daily remembrance that we are helping others for God. Pride would limit our vision by having us think or work for self, and not think and work for God through self and others.

Pride of Authority Is a Type of Pride

Pride of authority, or pride of superiority, is one form of excessive self-love. It expresses itself in thought or word or deed in a domineering, over-positive, offensive way. How overbearing it can be, how haughty, what a bully, how bossy, how prone to rule things! How critical it can be: "do unto others" is wholly or partially forgotten; the rights and feelings of others are given little or no consideration, for pride of authority is mean, unkind, disregarding justice and fair play and good sportsmanship. How argumentative and unreasonable it can be, for it loses sight of the true thought that "much might be said on both sides." Moreover, the argument is oftentimes forgotten in personal attack, or the defense of self is continued even when one knows that he is wrong but hates to admit it, and "e'en when vanquished he can argue still."[4] How given to anger pride of authority is! There is

---

[4] See Oliver Goldsmith, "The Village Schoolmaster."

no sweet reasonableness about it or in its methods; it is given to angry feelings, to angry thoughts, to angry speech, to angry acts.

From the following, each one can determine for himself whether pride of authority is his predominant fault:

Pride of authority is manifested by an overbearing attitude.

Have I a superior attitude in thinking or speaking or acting?

Am I snobbish?

Have I offensive, haughty ways of acting or carrying myself?

Do I hold myself above others?

Do I demand recognition?

Do I use the word *I* so much as to make it offensive?

Do I desire to be always first?

Do I seek advice?

Am I ready to accept advice?

Am I in any sense a bully?

Am I inclined to be bossy?

Am I prone to belittle persons, or places, or things?

What have I done to correct this overbearing attitude?

Pride of authority is manifested by a critical attitude.

Am I prone to be critical of persons, places, things?

Am I uncharitable?

Do I speak ill of others?

Have I lied about others?

Do I make known the faults of others?

Am I ready to speak about the faults of others?

Do I find fault easily?

Do I seek to place the blame on others, excusing myself?

Am I jealous?

Am I envious, wishing evil to another, rejoicing at his
    failures?

Am I quick to see the faults of others?

Do I ridicule others?

Am I inclined to make fun of others?

Do I listen to others who speak in a faultfinding way?

Do I refuse to see the good in others?

Do I carry small dislikes or even more-or-less serious ones?

Is there anyone to whom I refuse to speak?

Is there anyone to whom I have not spoken for a long
    time?

What have I done to correct this critical attitude?

Pride of authority is manifested by an argumentative attitude.

Am I prone to argue?

Am I positive and offensive in my arguments?

Have I a superior, a know-it-all attitude in arguments?

Is it my notion that others are usually or always wrong?

Do I refuse to give consideration to what they state?

Am I stubborn in my own defense?

Is it hard for me to yield a point?

Do I try to see both sides of a question?

Do I argue in my own defense, even when I know I am
    wrong?

Do I insist on having the last word?

Do I argue with anger, with personal animus, with
    uncharitableness?

Do I carry grudges or ill feeling on account of my
    arguments?

Have I tried to argue reasonably and without a raised tone?

What have I done to correct this argumentative attitude?

Pride of authority is manifested by an angry attitude.

Do I easily grow angry?

Have I an irritable disposition?

Do I lose my temper rather easily?

Does loss of temper make me sullen, unkind, uncharitable, critical?

Do I speak angrily?

Do I act angrily?

Do I try to control angry feelings?

Do I get angry because of opposition?

Am I so set on winning games that I get angry when losing?

Can I take part in a friendly argument without losing meekness?

Does a spiritual correction make me angry?

Do my mistakes make me angry?

Does a correction of any kind make me angry?

Is it a particular person, or place, or thing that arouses my temper?

What have I done to correct faults or sins against meekness?

Pride of Timidity Is a Type of Pride

Pride of timidity is self-love manifested by shyness, backwardness, cowardice. Pride of timidity is self-love protecting self through the hiding of weaknesses from fear of ridicule. Now, it must not be thought that the quiet person is necessarily humble. A fine reserve is praiseworthy, but timidity is carrying reserve to excess. Quietness of disposition may not show that there is pride beneath.

Ordinarily the talented are not so subject to pride of timidity, just because they are talented. Still those who have ability are not so generally developed as not to have some weakness or other, and even a strong weakness, as they view it. Self-love seeks to protect, to hide, that weakness and so develops a habit of timidity from it. Moreover, the talented are sometimes very much under the rule of human respect. They fear what others may say or think about them; they are in certain circumstances afraid to do what is right or to avoid what is wrong.

Nevertheless, pride of timidity is usually the predominant fault of those who have weaknesses and who seek to hide such weaknesses from fear of ridicule. Those who are governed by timidity are more or less under its spell in thought, word, and deed: when they pray, when they study or recite, when they work, when they play—in fact in anything that is done in a public way. They actually fear what others say or think about them; they remember things that have passed; they imagine what might happen; they picture improbable or almost impossible conditions or circumstances that will place them before the public eye. Day after day, in many small ways, they feel timid, and eventually it becomes a strong habit, so that they avoid, through human respect, what they should not avoid or do what they should not do.

Timidity, then, being a lack of confidence in self, brings irresolution. The timid make resolutions, but they have not the strength of will or the courage of heart to keep them. They feel discouraged because their fears are hard to overcome; their weaknesses seem so strong that they lose hope of any real and complete correction. They do not want to bear the unhappiness that such irresolution necessarily brings, yet they cannot keep up the fight day after day until they have brought timidity under complete control. True, they may suffer humiliations in the fight, but what is worth having is worth fighting for. Moreover, timidity is mostly a thing of the mind. Nervous, shy thinking means timid speaking or acting. If the will be made strong with resolution, timidity will soon be conquered.

From the following questions, each one can determine for himself whether pride of timidity is his predominant fault:

Do I think timidly?

Do I speak timidly?

Do I act timidly?

Have I shy eyes?

Have I a shy manner?

Have I a timid disposition?

Am I easily embarrassed?

Am I self-conscious?

Do I recognize my weaknesses as they really are?

Do I exaggerate them?

Do I try to hide them?

Am I dreadfully afraid that others may see them?

Do I fear ridicule because of them?

Am I shy about doing things in public?

Am I shy about singing in common?

Am I shy about reciting, speaking, reading in public?

Am I backward about serving in public?

Do I try to get out of things?

Do I compare my talents with those of others?

Do I seek to make full use of such talent as I have?

Do I understand that God has given me what I have?

Do I try to develop my talents?

Do I bury my physical, mental, or spiritual talents?

Am I so afraid of mistakes as not to try at all, or weakly?

Am I open and frank with my confessor, my spiritual
director?

Am I frank with my superior?

Does human respect enter into my daily life?

Do I wonder what others may say or think?

Am I afraid to be pious? obedient? charitable? humble? mortified?

Am I afraid to keep the rule?

Am I afraid to be studious?

Do I stay with the crowd—be it right or wrong?

Does shyness lead me into deliberate wrong?

Am I timid about playing games for fear I may do poorly, or even lose?

If I am not first, do I try to be second, or third, or fourth, and so forth?

Am I afraid to correct others?

Am I loyal to the Church, to principle, to this house?

Because of my timidity, do I carry grudges or ill feeling?

What have I done to correct pride of timidity?

Do I keep making resolutions?

Pride of Sensitiveness Is a Type of Pride

Pride of sensitiveness is brought about by self-love being wounded. The sensitive person is quickly hurt. In fact, it may be said, he prepares himself to be wounded. Ordinarily he imagines things, he misjudges, he misinterprets, he exaggerates, he is suspicious and distrustful. His memory is prone to cling to what has happened to him in an adverse way; he remembers who and what have hurt him. He is ready to see a slight and to feel it. He plans revenge. He fights mental battles of what he will say and how he will act. He is unforgiving, carrying ill feeling for short or long periods of time and, in the same mood, refusing to speak or speaking coldly to the one who is the object of his bitterness.

The sensitive person usually has a wild imagination. He imagines things; he creates improbable and almost impossible conditions; he pictures what may happen; and always he is being more or less wounded by someone. He feels that others do not make him welcome; he thinks they do not like him, or are trying to make fun of him, or are talking about him when he is absent. He imagines he is not wanted in games, and any mistakes he makes therein prove further to him that such is the case. His superior has a grudge against him; his teachers are not just; his companions are harsh and uncharitable. Seemingly nearly everybody is opposed to him. No wonder he is self-conscious; no wonder he is moody; no wonder he broods.

How unreasonable the sensitive person is! He is the cause to a great extent of his own unhappiness, though actually he gets malicious joy out of his sensitiveness at times. He knows that others realize that they must be on their guard how they speak or act to him, and that very consideration makes him more self-centered. If others hurt him, he is glad; he has someone to be offended at; another will have to bow in apology to him; there is a sense of satisfaction in not being on speaking terms with another. He makes himself feel bad; he wants to feel bad; he gets a false joy out of it. He does not seem to understand that suffering from the right motive brings happiness; he does not realize that he is only adding to his unhappiness — that such false joy as he allows himself is passing, unreasonable, and wrong.

The sensitive person is a source of unhappiness to others. He spreads his bitterness. He pulls down the morale of a house. To approach him is hard; to carry on a conversation with him is difficult; to live meekly in harmony with him is almost impossible. Corrections, advice, help, and favors he resents, disliking to admit weaknesses. Innocent fun at his expense is risky. Others have to make more than ordinary efforts to get along with him. The result is unhappiness.

The sensitive person should bear in mind that his sensitiveness is the cause of many falls and much unhappiness to himself and to others. All his powers should help him to correct this self-centered condition of soul.

From the following questions, each one can determine for himself whether pride of sensitiveness is his predominant fault:

Am I sensitive?

Am I easily wounded?

Do I think that others are always trying to hurt my feelings?

Am I suspicious, distrustful?

Do I misjudge or misinterpret others?

Am I ready to accuse others of being unjust or unfair to me?

Do I accuse others of being deliberately unkind to me?

Do I imagine things?

Do I imagine that others are willfully hurting me?

Do I allow innocent fun at my expense?

Do I laugh at my foibles? My mistakes?

Do I think that others do not like me?

Do I think that I am unwelcome in the company of others?

Am I unforgiving?

Do I carry grudges?

Do I refuse to speak to others?

Am I moody? Do I brood about things?

Am I hard to get along with?

Am I critical, unkind, deliberately uncharitable?

Have I a true consideration for others?

Do I act toward others as I want them to act toward me?

What have I done to correct pride of sensitiveness?

Am I willing to accept advice, correction, or help?

Pride of Complacency (Vanity) Is a Type of Pride

Pride of complacency is commonly called pride of vanity. It is self-love demanding self-esteem or the esteem of others. Yet it is not so much the self-esteem that is sought as it is the craving for the good opinion of others. That is, one suffering from this type of pride is anxious to be well thought of in regard to things spiritual, mental, or physical, so he thinks or speaks or acts vainly.

Pride of vanity, then, brings about a false motive of conduct, for he who labors for the esteem of others forgets that God bestows gifts of body and soul and that God gives the grace for the use of those gifts. God wants each one to acknowledge his debt. What does it profit to gain the esteem of others if one is forgetful of God? Why should anyone work from a false motive and thus spoil what would otherwise be good? What does vanity profit? Why not work for God, giving Him due credit? Why make self or others a motive of conduct?

It is true that humility is the truth about oneself. Nevertheless, he who is truly spiritual, or intellectual, or who lives up to a fine standard in general, or who is close to perfection, striving earnestly for it, could still be the subject of vanity. He may fail to recognize what God has given Him, or he could use his gifts in the wrong way. He could make his motive of conduct the esteem of others. It is also true that those who are far from gifted in any way can be under the spell of vanity, because of working for the esteem of others.

Vanity does not attack each and every one in the same way. That is, temptations to vanity may be in regard to spiritual or mental or physical affairs, to any two of the three, or to all three.

Rooting Out Hidden Faults

Vanity may precede, or accompany, or follow an act. Some are vain concerning things they are about to do, or things they would like to do, or things that are unreal—impossible and improbable dreams—that they cannot hope ever to do. Others are vain while they are performing an act; they want to make an impression; they are set on the effect that they are about to produce; the external reveals the internal; they are seeking the praise of the crowd; they aim to attract attention or to be noticed; they want to stand high and even first in public estimation. Still others are vain after they have done something; they think with self-praise about what they have accomplished; they glory in their own success; they color it; they exaggerate it; they speak about it; they seek the praise of others; they hint to get it or even speak openly to obtain it.

Certainly it is unreasonable to strive for goodness from a motive of vanity. It is wrong, of course. It is unreasonable to try to be obedient, or mortified, or charitable, or prayerful, or to love God for the esteem of others, though one can desire the good opinion of his superior, or confessor, or director for the sake of knowing that he is doing well and that he is on the right road. Yet it is sometimes true that the vain practice virtue, especially piety, so that they may be well thought of. It is also a fact that some who are leading good lives start to wonder foolishly about such goodness and exaggerate. They imagine they are better than they actually are, or they compare themselves with others. They seek to find out what is thought about the spiritual standards of others, thus hoping to find out what is thought about their own. They may even have ridiculous ideas concerning how good they are and, Pharisee-like, praise themselves and condemn others. They may go so far wrong as to imagine that they are very pleasing to God and then begin to develop peculiarities or oddities of conduct. They grow solemn and most recollected externally; they sigh and weep; they become sentimental; they act piously; they become imprudent in following the ordinary paths. They place goodness not in faithful service to God through daily affairs but in exceptional things, particularly devotions that attract the attention of others. In neglecting the lesser things, they are, in fact, falling into much wrong and consequently give a bad example. Their type of piety is offensive. Holiness suffers, for many who are not judges of true and false piety see this false type and decide they do not want to be good.

Vanity sometimes leads one to the practice of a particular virtue, to the neglect of other virtues. He who gets an exaggerated notion of one quality is apt to forget other qualities that are just as necessary. True goodness is the practice of many virtues, the neglect of none, though one virtue be more followed and acquired than others. There are some who are obedient yet uncharitable; others who are pious but critical; still others who are mortified and far from being humble. Now, it is not necessarily true that such persons are vain; however, the reverse is often true — the vain person is apt to insist on all virtues except the one he lacks, humility.

It is perhaps true that vanity in regard to mental talents, or the use of them, is more common than vanity in regard to spiritual affairs. There is something repelling in being good and at the same time being vain about it. The hypocrite who assumes what he has not is not so blind as to be wholly satisfied with self-sufficiency; he realizes that the esteem that he has gained is undeserved. Conscience reproaches him sooner or later. Conscience ordinarily does not reprove with the same intensity or even readiness when there is a question of vanity in regard to gifts of the mind. The brilliant, the very capable, may be attacked by this type of vanity, by self-glory, by exaggerating what they have, by working for the esteem of others. The mediocre may be attacked by self-glory, by exaggerating what they have, by working for the esteem of others. So may the untalented. The capable who are vain are readily subject to flattery and deceit; the mediocre who are vain feel the neglect of others; the untalented usually think that they are being treated unfairly. All are more or less sensitive, all to some extent are ridiculed, for the vain create opposition and dislike.

Vanity may attack concerning physical affairs. The vain parade their gifts; they glory in display; they endeavor to be noticed and well thought of in regard to looks, personal appearance, even strength or the lack of it. Now, there is no question that these are helps in daily life, but their importance can be exaggerated; they can be used from a wrong motive or for a wrong end. They stand for little if character is lacking; whereas, with character, they are aids to success. Of course, each one should be presentable: neat, clean, and modest; carelessness about personal appearance, boorishness, lack of order, slovenliness in manner or dress are rightfully to be condemned. Belittling the necessity of care of personal appearance is the opposite of attaching too much importance to it by being worldly, going beyond one's means, forgetting one's state of life, and so forth.

Vanity may attack one in regard to external conduct. If one is vain about prayers, he will seek external devotions, act piously, or strive to make an impression through the practice of virtue. He will keep rules to be observed; he will be recollected to attract attention; he will think of the good example he is giving. If one is vain about studies, he will manifest it in the way he thinks, or speaks, or acts; he will try to make a show of his knowledge; he will have much about him that is egotistical; he will have a spirit of contradiction; he will study and recite to gain further esteem of others. If one is vain about things of recreation, he will assume the attitude of a hero; he will wonder what impression he is making on the crowd. If one is vain about looks and personal appearance, he will show it by the nicety of the care that he gives to them.

The limits of vain thinking depend on each one. Herein is opportunity to let the imagination run wild into things possible or impossible, things probable or improbable, and the fanciful pictures always lead to the esteem of others. Vain thinking is stupid, unreasonable, and sinful, and the only one who can bring it under control is he who is tempted in that way. There is a limit to vanity of speech. Propriety and common sense are the check, for no one wants to be considered a boaster or a braggart. One who boasts usually avoids going to such limits as to be called a boaster; one may brag and exaggerate, yet he shuns being called a braggart. So one may lie (vanity is really lying); still he does not wish to be called a liar. One may seek praise; nevertheless he does not want others to think he is doing so. The vain, though very unreasonable about thinking vainly, are somewhat reasonable about speaking vainly. They realize that the one way not to gain the esteem of others is to be vain in speech, for vanity of speech does not attract; in fact, it repels; it makes unfriendliness. So does vanity in act or external conduct. The one who acts vainly or shows that he is vain is open to ridicule, flattery, and deceit, which means that he is losing the very thing he is after — namely, the esteem of others.

Ideals are not opposed to humility. To have a worthwhile goal and to seek for it is praiseworthy. The goal sought may never be reached, yet it keeps beckoning onward and upward, for steady purpose and persevering effort must bear fruit. The ideal will be above one's powers and there may be temptation to seek it from the wrong motive; nevertheless, when one recognizes his limitations and acts from a good motive, he is following our Lord's exhortation: "Be ye perfect." To do one's best, not to be satisfied with less than one's best, to strive for perfection in every sphere of life, should be one's aim. The important question is not whether or not one is perfect but what zeal is being used to reach perfection.

Of course, it is not vanity to guard a good name zealously. There is the obligation of preserving a reputation. Humility is a true love of self; to seek and to hold a good name would be a true love of self. Pride is an inordinate love of self and, hence, seeks the good opinions of others in an excessive way.

From the following questions, each one should be able to determine for himself whether pride of complacency is his predominant fault in spiritual affairs:

Am I vain in thoughts concerning spiritual affairs?

Am I vain in words in regard to spiritual affairs?

Am I vain in acts in regard to spiritual affairs?

Am I subject to vainglory?

Do I seek the esteem of others in regard to spiritual affairs?

Am I vain about my piety in public prayers?

Am I vain about my recollection? Meditation? Mass? Visits? Devotions?

Am I vain about my public prayer?

Am I vain about my rule keeping?

Am I vain about my prompt, cheerful, generous, supernatural obedience?

Am I vain about my charity?

Am I vain about my mortifications of the senses, especially taste?

Am I vain about any bodily mortification?

Am I vain about any mental mortification?

Am I vain about my avoidance of sin and imperfections?

Does vanity enter into my confessions? Directions?
   Monitions?

Am I vain about my general standard?

Am I vain about private devotions?

Have I an exalted opinion of my goodness?

Do I act piously? Seek strange devotions?

Has my piety made me odd?

Does my piety give offense to others?

Do I love to speak about my goodness?

Do I compare my goodness, my standard, to that of others?

Do I criticize the spiritual life of others?

Do I find fault with the way others practice virtue?

Am I prone to notice faults and to speak about them?

Do I misjudge others?

What effort have I made to be humble?

Do I realize that spiritual gifts come from God?

Do I understand that the use of spiritual gifts
   depends on God?

Do I give God credit for spiritual gifts and the use of them?

Am I anxious not to be vain about spiritual affairs?

Pride of vanity is manifested thus in regard to mental affairs.

Am I vain in thoughts concerning mental affairs?

Am I vain in words concerning mental affairs?

Am I vain in acts concerning mental affairs?

Am I subject to vainglory?

Do I have distractions of vainglory?

Do I daydream in a heroic way?

Do I seek the esteem of others in regard to mental affairs?

Am I vain about my memory?

Am I vain about my imagination?

Am I vain about my powers of reasoning?

Am I vain about my powers of understanding?

Do I seek to show my knowledge?

Do I ask questions for the purpose of showing my ability?

Have I a conceited way of explaining things to others?

Is vanity my motive for studying:

- Do I recite in a vain way?
- Do I seek to have others praise my accomplishments?
- Do I speak about my mental ability?
- Do I speak vainly about how much I study?
- Do I speak vainly about the amount of time I devote to study?

Through reasons of vanity, do I compare my standards to that of others?

Am I envious of the standard of others?

Am I anxious to surpass others?

What effort have I made to be humble?

Do I realize that mental ability comes from God?

Do I understand that the use of mental ability depends on God?

Do I give God due credit for my mental ability and the use of it?

Am I anxious not to be vain concerning mental affairs?

Pride of vanity is manifested thus in regard to external affairs.

Am I vain in act?

Is my conduct vain?

Am I vain about looks?

Am I vain about my personal appearance?

Am I vain in the way I walk?

Am I vain in the way I speak?

Is my manner vain?

Do the very tones of my voice reveal vanity?

Am I vain about health? Strength?

Am I vain about my reading in public?

Am I vain about reciting in public?

Am I vain about singing?

Am I vain in the display of my talents?

Am I vain in my games?

Do I play to make an impression on others?

Is my attitude in games one of vanity?

Do I seek praise?

Am I anxious to be humble?

Do I give God credit for His gifts?

Do I try to use these gifts in the right way?

Do I strive to give God credit for the use of His gifts?

How to Overcome Pride

Prayer changes pride to humility. Too often it is thought that the gaining of a virtue depends on human effort alone. Grace is necessary to acquire virtue, and grace comes through prayer. Surely we understand that God is willing to help us, for He wants us to be humble. Pray for humility, then, as though all depended on prayer; labor for humility, then, as though all depended on human effort alone.

Meditating on humility will help us to acquire it. Pride has been punished; the examples are so many and so well known that they need not be mentioned. Moreover, pride has been condemned and humility extolled; Our Lord, on different occasions, praised the latter and censured the former. Humility was the virtue that stood out in the life of our Lord and the virtue that the saints had in a marked degree. Knowing the above to be true, each one should endeavor to understand why humility is so praiseworthy. Humility is a true knowledge of self. It is the truth about oneself. It is as we are in the sight of God. It is the recognition that our gifts come from God and the use of them depends on God. God, all; self, nothing. God, the Giver of all, to whom all is due; self, the receiver, who should acknowledge dependence on God.

Of course, we should not expect to acquire a habit of humility all at once. Habits come after repeated acts. Moreover, it takes time to destroy a habit of pride, more time if that habit is deeply rooted or the result of long growth. A steady purpose and persevering effort sooner or later must be rewarded. There may be temptations to lose heart, but nothing worthwhile is gained except through constancy. Pray that the effort be steady and persevering. Keep in mind that God is helping you with His grace.

Pride is changed to humility through acts of humility and the acceptance of humiliations. Make frequent acts of humility and accept the humiliations of daily life. There are many details that can be cheerfully borne, not only the slight mistakes or small failures in games or studies or in spiritual affairs, but also uncharitable statements, corrections, and misunderstandings. All of us are prone to make excuses for ourselves, to defend ourselves, to urge our opinions, even with anger or uncharitableness. It should be perfectly obvious that unless humiliations are accepted, there can be no true progress in the virtue that is sought, for the very materials that should be used are thrown aside. It should also be reasonably clear that when one accepts the humiliations that fall to his lot, he is learning to be humble, for as obedience comes by obeying, or mortification through mortification, or prayerfulness through prayer, so humility is acquired through the practice of humility, by making acts of humility and by accepting humiliations. When one fully accepts the humiliations that come by chance, then one is ready to seek humiliations. Prudent direction should govern anyone seeking humiliations.

Study yourself. What type of pride attacks you most? Does it arise because of persons or places or things? Determine the detail that should be corrected. Do not choose something that is general; do not attempt to do too much at one time or in a short while. Do something every day. In other words learn the particular source of pride that is attacking and let the resolution be practical by making it as particular as possible. Repeat that resolution many times during the day; let it be in the thoughts at rising and on through the day until retiring.

To avoid an overbearing spirit, renew the determination to kill any spirit of contradiction, any spirit of superiority, any temptation not to live in harmony with others. Strive to be friendly with everybody; seek to be considerate of others; "be all in all to all"; be agreeable and pleasant. To avoid anger, learn to be meek by repressing the first movements of anger; endeavor not to allow angry feelings to arise; never speak when under the influence of anger. Let there be a constant resolution to live peacefully with others, no matter how much self-restraint is needed. To avoid criticism, see the good in everybody. A study of others will reveal that they have good qualities. Recognize that we all have defects and hence should bear with the defects of others. Acquire a spirit of justice; be fair to each and every one; be ready to give others credit for what they do. Praise when praise is due. Do not allow false judgments to become a rule. To be charitable, say to yourself that you are going to take the full responsibility of being considerate of others, of getting along well with others, and regardless of how they act or speak, you are going to be mindful of the great virtue of charity.

To avoid timidity, oppose it, act against it, do not give in to it. Timidity, shyness, backwardness, self-consciousness, and cowardice are really mental — that is, the thoughts are timid and hence the speech and acts are because of what others will say or think. Timidity in general arises from fear of appearing or doing things before others. Confidence in self is simply a matter of training; resolve not to be timid or nervous, and soon you will not be. Kill the fear of praying, reciting, singing, and playing before others; destroy that fear by meeting others without embarrassment. Why care what others say or think? Others may be more gifted, but what of that? Learn by making mistakes, if necessary. Do not place the burden on yourself of being first, or second, or third, or in any particular place, for that matter; there are different degrees of glory. Use fully what gifts you have, even though they are small. Bear the mortifications and humiliations that may arise. Just because you are not among the leaders, just because you are not as gifted as others, do not be satisfied to be the last. Be content to place yourself where you belong and try to improve. God expects each one of us to use what gifts he has. The more gifted you are, the more resolved should you be to fight down timidity, which would keep you from using such gifts.

To overcome sensitiveness ask yourself a few questions: "Why should I allow myself to be sensitive? It offends God; it makes me unhappy; it spreads unhappiness. I am going to study the cause of my sensitiveness. I know that I most readily take offense from certain persons; I realize that I feel out of place or unwelcome in certain places; I understand that I am quick to be hurt by corrections, mistakes, criticism, a sense of inferiority, lack of ability, small failures—in fact, almost anything. I am not going to allow myself to be sensitive; I am resolved that I will not be hurt; I will restrain my feelings; I will bear with that which formerly would wound me." Such a resolution will quickly show results and, if perseveringly kept, perfect success.

To overcome pride of vanity we should realize that what he have received from God and the use of what we have depends on God. We should learn to give Him credit for our talents and the use of them; we should not take the credit to ourselves. We should learn to live for Him; we should strive to pray, study, play, work, and do all for Him, making Him the motive of our daily life. Any virtue implies forgetfulness of self: obedience is the submission of one's will to that of another; mortification is bringing self into subjection; love of neighbor is consideration for another; prayer is thinking about God, while talking to Him; hence vanity should be corrected so as to bring about a state of mind and conduct that has God as the motive. Is it not reasonable to make God the end of our thoughts, and words, and deeds? Is it not spiritual and, therefore, a source of happiness? Is it not a sure means of progress? Then why not give God credit for what we have and do? "All for Thee, my God"; "All for Thee, O my Jesus."

Pray to be humble; let the effort be steady and persevering; make acts of humility and accept the humiliations of daily life; study yourself; let your resolutions be practical by being particular; keep in mind the type of pride that is being attacked; repeat your resolution often. Pray as though all depended on prayer; labor as though all depended on human effort alone.

Chapter 7

∞

Avarice as a Predominant Fault

Avarice is an inordinate love of worldly goods. It refers to the desire for riches as well as to the wish to possess things.

Those who are following a vocation and who have not a vow of poverty are expected to be poor in spirit. What does *vocation* mean? Using one's state of life for personal profit? Piling up money? Becoming attached to places or things? Setting one's heart on certain appointments? "Blessed are the poor in spirit: for theirs is the Kingdom of Heaven" (Matt. 5:3). The glory of God suggests prudent detachment.

Herein, however, there is question of avarice as a predominant fault, as it applies to those who have a vow of poverty or who are preparing to take such a vow, which demands a renunciation of earthly goods and interior detachment from the same.

We all have a tendency to acquire and to use things. We want ownership, or at least we desire the use of certain earthly things. The vow of poverty does not of itself do away with the tendency, but it does seek to regulate it through exterior and interior renunciation. This very surrender, this endeavor to control a tendency, can be looked upon as a burden, or a yoke, or a restraint — a sort of "how far can one go and still not violate the vow" attitude. Of course, it is readily understood that merely to seek to keep the letter of the vow and not to be concerned about its spirit is reaching for the day when the letter will mean "stop on this side of something serious."

The vow is an offering. It is taken as a means to salvation and holiness; it should also be a way of doing God's work better through others. It is giving God something. Consequently, the first thought should not be burden but sacrifice. There should be a generous will in the surrender; there should be joy in what is being done; the gift should be wholehearted and complete. In fact, one should not only accept the opportunities to practice poverty but also seek other means to be poor in spirit. The thought should be not how much the vow of poverty imposes but how much can one do to carry out the vow fully? Living poverty means practicing poverty. The vow should stand for that. There should be joy in not having; there should be happiness in doing without; there should be content of heart in not wanting. Renunciation and detachment, the more perfect they are, the more fully practiced, are so much more the bringers of true joy. What does poverty mean to you? Is it a burden, a yoke, a restraining obligation? Or is it a generous giving up of ownership and of the will to have? Is your state of mind one that is poor in spirit?

The ordinary temptation for those who have the vow of poverty is not to be detached from earthly things. They can allow their affections to be unduly strong for persons or places or things. They can want the things that they have not and which they could easily forgo. They can sigh for the very things that they have renounced. They can have a false attachment for home, for amusements, for books, for furniture, for costly or precious things that do not fit their state of life. Besides desiring things that they have not, they can become strongly attached to things that they actually have. No matter how small the thing in question, they can have an undue regard for it; correspondingly the undue regard could very likely be true in question of things of more importance. They could fail to be detached concerning an act of obedience, a place to live, a room, things that are for their use, and even in regard to things of little value, holy pictures, medals, prayer books, or even more trivial things. The tendency to exercise ownership may be constantly present; the wish to have things, the desire to use things and to keep them for personal use, may be ever at hand. Detachment keeps such tendencies in check.

Poverty allows what is necessary. Necessity differs for the individual; simply because one has something is no reason why another should think he needs the same thing. What one needs is not what another needs. Still, there is always the chance of allowing oneself to be fooled as to what is necessary. Reasonableness is one guide; prudence is another; the will of the superior and custom are also guides. The spirit of poverty will be safeguarded if the will of the superior is accepted fully and joyfully. To be ready to accede to what the superior thinks is necessary is to have a state of mind that accepts the idea and spirit of the vow. It need not be said that there are varying degrees of necessity. Some things that are expedient can be reasonably done without; other things cannot be had unless one acts unreasonably. Let conscience and the will of the superior be the guides.

Certainly poverty is not slovenliness. The dignity of our state of life must be maintained. We should protect the respect that is due teachers and leaders. We cannot afford to be careless in this matter. Nevertheless, though we do hold to the spirit of the vow as regards clothes, furniture, the things we have for our use, and so forth, is our state of mind in accord with our practice? Are we truly detached? Do we want that which we have not? Are we glad to be poor in spirit and yet neat, clean, and orderly?

Poverty is not miserliness, which seeks to acquire, to save, to hoard. The attachment to things is such that not only is there a reaching out for more, but there is also an unwillingness to give up what one has. Possession becomes a passion spreading even to those things that are not worth keeping or that will go to waste by being kept. Stinginess offends against charity as well as the vow of poverty. To cling to things is to feed avarice. A spirit of generosity is of help in keeping the vow of poverty, for the generous person readily relinquishes the use of things and so has no desire to keep things for self, has no desire to use things for self. However, it must be remembered that poverty is a taking care of things. What we have and what we use, we should guard. Not only should we protect what is set aside for our personal use, but we should also be concerned about those things intended for common use, and so far as we can, we should teach others to protect those same things.

Poverty, then, is the means to keep regulated and normal the tendency to want to own things and to have a personal use of things; avarice, an inordinate desire for earthly things, is very often mere selfishness. Poverty holds in check our love of worldly things; it controls the desire of ownership; it regulates the use of things. Above all, it sets a state of mind that is attracted to poverty in spirit. Poverty seeks to make us detached by having us be generous in our surrender of worldly things, by having us satisfied with the obligations that it imposes, by having us joyous in offering more, by having us ready to accept new and happy yokes, by having us detached as completely as possible, even to perfection.

From the following, each one should determine for himself whether avarice is his predominant fault:

Have I an inordinate love of worldly goods?

Have I an immoderate desire of earthly things?

Do I regret that I cannot get them?

Do I want to own things?

Do I see what others have and want the same?

Have I sought to control the tendency to avarice?

Is the vow of poverty a burden to me? Or is the vow of poverty an offering, a gift, a surrender?

Do I try to observe the vow fully?

Am I careless about details?

Do I break the vow in small ways? Frequently? Habitually?

Do I have the proper permission for what I receive or give?

Do I use things reasonably?

Am I miserly in hoarding things?

Do I cling with too much affection to necessary things?

Do I hold to things with stubbornness?

Am I willing to give up what has been set aside for my use?

Do I want what is costly in clothes?

Do I want what is costly or too precious in books, furniture, and so forth?

Is my room neat, clean, and orderly?

Do I think in terms of ownership?

Do I think about acquiring things?

Do I speak in a way that shows I have a tendency to avarice?

Do I act in a way that shows a tendency to avarice?

Am I selfish?

Do I seek unnecessary things?

Do I feel bad in bearing the effects of poverty?

Do I complain?

What is my state of mind?

Have I made a real renunciation of worldly things?

Am I detached?

Could I be more detached?

How to Overcome Avarice

To be poor in spirit, pray. Prayer is the one great help in acquiring any virtue, and hence it must be used to kill the tendency to avarice and to become detached. To preserve poverty, meditate on the poverty of Our Lord; "What shall it profit a man, if he gain the whole world, and suffer the loss of his soul?" (Mark 8:36). Above these, and yet with them, practice poverty. Seek to be perfectly detached. Shun in thought and word and deed anything that would be a giving in to the tendency to avarice. Learn to be poor by being poor. Make the renunciation complete. Let the offering of poverty be a generous gift. Let us use what is necessary, but let us not set our hearts on anything. Wish and pray that the will of God may be entirely fulfilled through the practice of poverty.

Chapter 8

∞

Lust as a Predominant Fault

"Who shall ascend into the mountain of the Lord: or who shall stand in the holy place? The clean of heart, for they shall see God" (Ps. 23:3). "Blessed are the clean of heart: for they shall see God" (Matt. 5:8). Now, it should be remembered that by "cleanness of heart" is meant not only the avoidance of serious sins against the angelic virtue, but also the keeping from venial sin and imperfections that sooner or later draw us into grave temptation. Surely all of us should strive to have perfect modesty in all things.

We know what God wants in this regard. We realize the malice of mortal sin and especially the serious malice of degrading sins against the angelic virtue. We understand the shame that is attached to such sins, whether they be in thought, word, or deed. We know that temptations may come, for there are at times signs of rebellion. The mind and the senses seek to pull down; war must be waged against them. Guards must be placed so that they do not fall into that which is unlawful. They can have the right kind of liberty, but it must not descend to license. They should be regulated; they should be brought into perfect subjection.

Rooting Out Hidden Faults

The sense of touch should be strictly regulated, because, as St. Thomas says, it is the foundation of all the other senses. This regulation should be most exacting in regard to self and others. What may seem light and even innocent, sooner or later tends to sin and serious sin. Therefore, all softness of conduct and all signs of effeminacy should be avoided, such as the too frequent shaking of hands, hanging on to one another, anything that looks like caressing, going around arm in arm, hands on one another. In regard to self, one cannot be too severe. The saints were very strict in the regulation of this sense. They brought themselves into complete subjection by acts of self-denial or of mortification or through the wearing of hair shirts or chains; they inflicted punishment on themselves by using the discipline. We can and should profit by their example, though prudence and the rule demand that we do practically nothing in bodily mortification without the advice of our superior, confessor, or spiritual director.

The sense of taste should also be brought under control. If the taste is unruly, then almost surely will there be less than true modesty. The quality and quantity of things eaten or drunk must be according to right reason; excesses should always be avoided; delicacies used prudently and sparingly. Fasting is one way of regulating the taste; abstinence is another; nevertheless, fasting, or complete abstinence from anything, should not be done without due permission. Still, each one can mortify himself by crossing his taste, by taking a little less of something and especially of things pleasant and agreeable. Moreover, there can be self-denial in the way that one thinks or speaks or acts about things to eat or drink. Mortification makes one reasonable.

The tongue, as the organ of speech, should be brought into subjection. The language of a modest man is modest. Speech should have that refinement, that spirit that signifies the presence of Christ; what could not be said to Him should not be said at all. So there should be avoided anything that savors of softness in speech — the use of terms of endearment, love terms, the singing of worldly love songs. The tongue should control any tendency to softness of character. Moreover, the tongue should not be given to false humor; fun should not be vulgar or sinful. The spirit of Our Lord should ever be present.

The ears should be held in restraint. True modesty and unregulated ears do not go together. To allow the ears undue liberty is to be careless about the spirit of the holy virtue, for things heard can and do leave strong impressions. Prudence and good judgment must be the guide. What one would not think or speak one should not listen to others say. Listen to nothing that is offensive to good taste.

The eyes should be guarded. The soul must not permit sins and imperfections to enter "through the windows"; nor should it allow itself to become "the prey of the eyes." An appeal to the eyes is being made at the present day, for they are prone to be unruly and curious; they seek the sensible, and if habit has made them unguarded, they go further, modesty and reserve being sacrificed. The eyes love to wander; they want to see; they are attracted not only to the good but also to that which is not good; they delight in the unusual, the startling, the alluring, for they want to be entertained and amused. And, willing or unwilling, they print pictures on the imagination that memory easily brings back. Consequently, there should be carefulness to a detail in keeping the eyes under control in regard to self and others, in regard to pictures and reading, in regard to anything that might offend modesty, for if they are unruly, they prevent spiritual progress and urge spiritual decline. The eyes are wonderful gifts, but they easily become deadly enemies.

The mind, as well as the senses, should be brought under control. A mind that is given to daydreaming and wandering, to lack of attention, is not modest; liberty is not license. It is just as possible to develop a state of mind that is modest as to develop one that is otherwise. The mind will not be any more regulated than the senses, so it stands to reason that if the senses are dutifully controlled, the mind is also.

The heart — that is, the affections — should be regulated. Human affections are prone and oftentimes very prone to be unruly. Love is a great gift. It can be given to places or things or persons. It can go wrong and woefully; it can descend low and very low. Surely those who follow the Master should not seek their happiness in giving and receiving irregulated love. Their love should be broad, all-embracing. Their human friendship should be for all. Their supernatural love should be given to God. If God is truly loved, then all human affections will be regulated by that supernatural love. "Let us begin to love God a little"; let us be friends of everybody.

Those who follow the Master should seek to be modest in all things. As a great spiritual writer has said: "Imagine to yourself that you hear Him [Our Lord] say to His followers, 'Perform your outward actions after the manner in which I performed all of them; behave with that composure, modesty, decency, caution, with that fitness and gentleness wherewith I behaved on earth!'"

Let us examine our consciences in regard to the following:

Are my senses being brought under control gradually?

Is my mind being brought under control?

Am I growing more and more attentive?

Which sense should be denied most: Sight? Hearing? Taste? Touch? Smell?

With what zeal have I tried to bring my mind and senses
under control?

With what zeal have I tried to make them perfect?

Am I modest to a detail? In regard to self and others?

Do I realize that spiritual progress depends on control of
the mind and the senses?

Do I realize that progress in studies depends on control of
the mind and the senses?

Is modesty one virtue that I keep perfect?

Pray to Acquire Modesty

There is no fact so emphasized in Scripture and Tradition as
the necessity of prayer. Scripture repeatedly commands that it
be constant, frequent, even daily: "Watch ye, and pray.... Pray
always" (Matt. 26:41; 2 Thess. 1:11). Tradition, the record of the
ages, the history of the saints, and the life of the faithful are an
unceasing exhortation to pray. No age is without its testimony
to the necessity of prayer.

To acquire perfect modesty, to acquire any virtue, pray. Life
is a warfare, a battle. The greatest battles have been fought, not
on fields reddened with blood, but in the soul, where the battle
is intensified by the powerful forces of good and evil striving for
the priceless gift of God—the human soul. The history of the
soul shows records of success and failure, for souls, generation
after generation, have been fighting a battle that is constant,
that death alone ends, and that is vitally important—a battle
not against flesh and blood, not against brothers in Christ, but
against principalities and powers, against the rulers of the world
of darkness, against the wickedness of the archfiend, who holds
at high command the very elements of daily life to wage the
deadly conflict.

The gifts of God can be employed by the individual soul for its own good or for its destruction. Those very powers that God gave to ensure salvation can be used to make eternal loss possible. The soul feels the waves of angry passion; it discovers the law of the mind; it finds the flesh lusting against the spirit. It realizes that the faculties of the mind — the memory, understanding, reason, imagination, free will — can awaken elements of strife; it understands that the senses can arouse the latent enemy.

How subdue the waves of angry passion? How control the law of the members ever pulling down? How bring the flesh into subjection? How combat seductive charms? It cannot be by merely physical means; it cannot be by natural power alone; it cannot be by any force except the spiritual, for the resistance must be superior to that used by the enemy. The attack and defense must be one of prayer. The prayerful man can move mountains; the prayerful man can do all things. No one denies that the battle may sometimes be hard, but only the coward succumbs; and it should be remembered that any virtue can be had if we pray for it, and the harder we pray, the sooner it will come.

Today is the time of high resolution, if you have not been faithful to prayer as the means of acquiring virtue. Today is the time to pray and pray hard, having confidence. Today is the time to begin prayers that will have perseverance until the goal is reached.

To acquire the virtue of modesty perfectly: watch, pray, fight, persevere. Avoid persons, places, and things that may mean temptation. Mortify the mind and the senses. Be frank with your spiritual director and confessor. Practice devotions to the Blessed Virgin, St. Joseph, and the other saints. Think of death and eternity. Go to Confession regularly. Receive Communion according to rule. Avoid idleness. Read spiritual books. Love Our

Lord. Keep close to Him in the Blessed Sacrament. Be zealous in trying to be good.

Love Others and Things in God

Our love should be given to God. He who loves God has an abiding sorrow for sin, for he remembers that he has offended God. God wants our love. He wants us to render a perfect service through that love. We should love God, for He has been good to us. We should love God because He is God.

Love can be given to other things. Love of the world is ruinous. The world is attractive; it is alluring; it can become irresistibly enticing, for it holds joy, good times, amusements. To give up the world and be with it in thought is unreasonably wrong. God or the world—which? True happiness or false? To have a vocation and to be worldly is to place a check on spiritual progress, is to rush into spiritual decline, is to have a vocation and not live it.

To love the world is ordinarily to love the pleasures of the world. We all want happiness; we all seek happiness; we all desire relaxation and recreation. Joy, amusement, and fun are a part of our natural life and should be a part of our supernatural life. Yet we can seek these outside the life to which we are called. We can be dissatisfied with the joy proper to our state of life. We can become so discontented as to make the pleasures of the world part of our life. We can allow a normal, natural tendency to be abnormal. We can find ways and means to go into the world, excusing ourselves by reason of more or less necessity. Let a false love of pleasure take hold, and the end is having a vocation but not living it, and the final result is refusing the hundredfold for following the Master.

Love can be thrown away on intellectual pursuits. Learning, culture, scholarships are much to be desired and much to be worked for. Books are an end thereto; they can be too absorbing; they can develop a taste that goes beyond the proper bounds. Study can become irregulated and bring about forgetfulness of other duties. Strive to be scholarly, but do not forget what the crucifix stands for. Scholarship, yes; nevertheless, not for self alone, but for the glory of God, the saving and making holy our souls, the salvation and holiness of others. Learning should not be for self alone; it is to fulfill more faithfully and in a higher way the duties of our state of life.

Much less should our love be cast away by being too attracted to sports. Recreation should help us to keep physically fit. Undue interest is harmful. We should not have an abnormal attraction for the games that we have taken part in or the ones that we shall take part in. Moreover, we should be on our guard that our interest in sports does not become irregulated, so that our joys or sorrows are bound in the success or failure of our favorites. Prudence should be the guide.

Above all, our love for others should be spiritual. Love is a great gift. Naturally, each one desires affection; naturally, each has a tendency to strive for the whole love of another, giving his own in return. There comes a time when human affections awaken strongly. Then there is a searching for someone who is to be a "best friend"; there is a seeking for someone who will be a best friend in return. Finally, the affections, after going hither and yon or even before, fall on one and remain there. Similar attractions, admiration, common sympathy, or any number of things increase the affection. True and perfect spiritual friendships are rare; particular friendships are dangerous and sinful. Strong human friendships for those following a vocation result in temptations to give and take signs of affection. Fire burns and leads to temptations; the path is downward, unhappy, much to be regretted, for the fruits are jealousy, uncharitableness, discord, improprieties, lack of community spirit. There is no limit to the depths to which false love and irregulated friendship goes. God has called us to His service and wants our love in a special way. We should love Him; He loves us. He alone can fill our craving for affection; He alone can keep our love whole and give His whole love in return; He alone can make it rise higher and higher to purer and better things. Love Him and love all through Him by being all to all.

Chapter 9

∞

Anger as a Predominant Fault

Anger is a disorderly emotion of the soul that inclines us to repel whatever displeases us and that leads us to revenge. However, there is a lawful anger, which is brought on by zeal for the honor of God. "Anger arising from zeal is virtuous, but the anger arising from passion is sinful," St. Gregory states. Anger arising from passion is what is meant in the following.

Anger is sinful and therefore an offense against God. We all understand that fact—anger offends a person; anger offends God. But we seldom stop to consider that anger has a reaction, an effect on him who indulges in it. That reaction, that effect, is unhappiness. Furthermore, anger has an effect on others; it is a source of unhappiness to others. For the sake of getting a new viewpoint about anger, or for the sake of bringing to mind something that may have been forgotten, let us, for the moment, not consider anger an offense against God, but let us follow the thought that anger is unreasonable because it brings unhappiness to self and others.

Most persons have temptations to anger. There is hardly anyone who does not at times become peevish, irritable, or impatient; and these are the beginnings of more serious faults. Now we all know the harm and very serious results of anger. There is no example that makes clearer its ruinous effects than the Crucifixion of Our Lord; there it had full and fatal fling; there it was a very strong disorderly emotion of soul that was satisfied only with the putting to death. We have also seen how anger has brought families into discord and even permanent separation. We have read how nations have been led into war. The surprising fact is that though each and every one has had brought to his attention the fruits of anger — the sufferings, the discord, the unhappiness — still there is much that could be sought by most persons in regard to meekness and something of meekness that could be sought by everybody.

The unhappy effect of anger on one who is given to it infrequently is not as great as the unhappy effect on him who falls often. Consequently, the unhappy effect of anger on others is ordinarily proportionate to the number of times one allows temper to be a master. Now, would you not think that everybody would be most unwilling to permit himself to be the cause of his own unhappiness, no matter how slight? And is he not more and more unreasonable as he allows himself more and more to be the cause of increasing unhappiness? Each one should have enough interest in himself so as to take the means to be rid of the source of that which stands for loss of peace of mind. Should not such a one be selfish enough to repress the first movement of anger? There are usually signs that it is rising; if one thinks angrily, he will soon speak or act angrily. Should not each one strive to get along well with everybody? We are not easily wounded by our friends; the very reason that we have friends is that we do not give vent to those things that would hurt them. Should not each one keep in check those bits of criticism, faultfinding, anything that destroys or lessens charity? What is so foolish as to be unhappy, when one of the sources of unhappiness could be cut off? What is so absurd as to make ourselves deliberately and willfully unhappy?

There is nothing finer than a happy family spirit. Anger tends to kill the right kind of community spirit. One person can drag others down very swiftly; anger has quick and often lasting fruits. How much unhappiness one chronically inclined person spreads we do not know and cannot reckon; there is no measure of sin that is exact; we do not understand the full effects of the Passion and death of Our Lord. What we do know is that one who is frequently given to anger does create discord and discontent, and partially or wholly tears down a happy family spirit. The breeding of discord by just one person can have far-reaching effects. Yet let us suppose that there is no one individual tearing down the happiness of others in a family; and let us imagine, therefore, that there is no one person given to frequent or serious faults of anger. Still, the fact of the matter is that small bits of anger by many could have the same effect of destroying happiness. Considered in itself, the bit of temper of one is small, but where many are gathered together and given to the same wrong, the effect is large and undesirable. Each bit of anger means unhappiness; unhappiness brings further unhappiness and further anger. That is why it is so important for each and every one to strive to acquire that perfect meekness that makes for a spirit of true happiness. Family spirit really depends on the individual, and no one should be willing to be the cause of another's unhappiness and wrong, for that other's unhappiness and wrong usually mean further unhappiness and wrong, and the end of it all we do not know and cannot reckon.

Whatever a person does goes into his character. Each act of virtue, regardless of how small it may be, goes into the forming and final makeup of character. Where the acts of virtue outnumber the acts of sin, the character is that much more virtuous.

Perfect character is perfect virtue. Saints are saints because they had so few faults and those are so very, very small. The most repulsive characters are formed by sin. Satan does nothing that is good. Now it will be seen that sin, since it is put into one's character, must have an effect on others. The sin of Judas had a tremendous and terrible effect; yet it must be remembered that any number of small sins that Judas fell into did not seem to have an effect on others; only the final big sin is taken into consideration. There is really no person who does not have some influence on some other person; that influence may be small, but, great or small, it is an influence. Now, where the influence is evil, unhappiness will result. Will you allow anger to grow more and more into your character, or will you foster meekness? There is unhappiness in the former; happiness in the latter. Will you permit your anger to be an influence on others, pulling them down and making them unhappy? Do you want to be unreasonable?

As a sort of business proposition, is it not worthwhile to keep from anger? Is not happiness worth working for? Should not each one be so concerned about his own joy as to be unwilling to allow himself to be the cause of his own unhappiness? Should not each one be considerate enough of the happiness of others to make strong efforts to preserve it? Let not anger make us unreasonable; let us not spread unhappiness.

Anger is unreasonable because it offends God. He loves us; He died for us; He is our best friend. Shall we be so foolish as to do what He begs us not to do? Shall we not be reasonable in seeking our happiness with God in doing what He wills?

Meekness

Even temper, the holding of anger in check, is the bringing of self-love into subjection. Life is such that each one is more or less on the lookout for self—not exactly with selfish interests or motives, but with the concern that one's first duty is to self. Consequently, whatever affects self is thought of, often spoken about, or even acted in some way or another.

Spiritually we all have our difficulties. We should not allow these difficulties to affect us in such a way as to take away our equability of temper. Self-restraint is needed, of course, to hold within bounds those things that may be more or less a bother or worry to us. We should not bemoan ourselves to others; we should not sadden or take the joy from life for those about us. We should be prepared to keep in check those things that may be causing us some trouble. More than this, we should be anxious to keep subdued those bits of bad humor that we all have at times. No one is so constantly joyous as not to feel out of sorts at times, and consequently no one should be surprised that such bits of bad humor try to have their satisfaction by being spent on others.

Meekness is spiritual; meekness is joy. And we should all strive to have in our hearts that joy that is contagiously cheerful. We need not think that we must be continually joking; nor should we believe that even-temperedness must express its happiness in laughter. We may and undoubtedly will have bothersome worries, but we can and should be even-tempered, retain our peace of heart, be meek in spite of them. We can at least bear with life's small problems in such a way as not to allow them to rush upon others.

Even temper is attractive, helps the community spirit, keeps down all that tends to anger, for it seeks under varying circumstances to be pleasant, amiable, agreeable, mild, patient. It is, in fact, the practice of many virtues. Call it personality, if you will, or say that it is the getting along well with others through a constant and insistent practice of charity. Regardless of how it is termed, it has charm and a very great deal of charm. It is winning; it is friendly; it attracts friends and holds them, while at the same time it makes friendly those who may, for some or no reason, entertain a slight dislike. Businessmen realize how valuable even-temperedness is, for it is the one quality they seek to be faithful to. They try to be agreeable to all with whom they trade, because they know that business will suffer if they offend by lack of the little civilities and courtesies of everyday life. They really go out of their way to attract and to hold customers. They would say that it is good business. Theirs might be called the natural side of even-temperedness, yet it could be that they are practicing the virtue of charity simply because of the happiness it brings them and spreads to others because it is pleasing to God.

We cannot measure the faults that arise through the lack of even-temperedness. Anger and its fruits — irritability, faultfinding, criticism, peevishness, uncharitableness — spread discord and discontent. Not that anyone deliberately aims to do this; nevertheless, the result is there. It is sufficiently bad that we should fall into such faults, but why should we be willing that others suffer from them? Reasonable thinking would suggest that if others are affected by what we do, then still others will be affected by what we have started. The full effect we certainly cannot hope to measure.

We should not be willing to allow others to say that we are hard to get along with. We should try to be the same; we should be even-tempered; we should keep the risings of anger under control. We should not be up and down, joyous and sad, silent and talkative, bubbling over with fun and decidedly morose. We must learn not to be changeable. Surely there are some with whom we live in joyous harmony. Is that harmony, that spirit of unity, that spirit of friendship because of them or because of us? Who should get the credit? It is almost equally true that we find it hard to get along with certain others, or perhaps a certain one. Who is responsible here? This person may have his faults just as we have, but have we not faults that repel him? Have we tried, seriously and with constant and daily effort, to be even-tempered? Have we tried to be pleasant and agreeable with everybody? Have we been so concerned about getting along well with everybody that we pray that such may be? And, at the same time, do we do all we can to subdue ourselves and especially the emotion of anger?

All this is very important where many are living together. One who is given to anger, who lacks evenness of temper, can do much harm; several could easily bring about almost complete ruin of community spirit. Each one must be convinced that he has a necessary part in helping others to keep the right and therefore spiritual kind of unity. This is a responsibility, a duty. Charity demands it. Not to accept this duty is to be indifferent to one's own happiness, is to be careless about one's standard; not to accept this responsibility is to be negligent in charity toward one's neighbor; not to accept this obligation is to be thoughtless and careless about the offense offered to God through the many faults and sins that most surely do arise.

Let us examine our consciences in regard to the following:

Am I prone to anger?

Do I have daily temptations to anger?

What seems to cause the temptation? A person? a place?

When do the temptations arise? During study? In class? At work? During recreation?

Does practically any little thing arouse me to temper?

Do I think angrily?

Do I lack evenness of temper in thought?

Is my state of mind an angry one?

Rooting Out Hidden Faults

Do I think complainingly? Critically? Faultfindingly?
Am I what is generally termed a sorehead?
Do I repress the first signs of anger?
Do I try to keep my soul in meekness?
Do I strive to get along well with everybody?
Do I ponder over slights or injuries and even
    presume them?
Am I easily disturbed in mind?
Am I easily wounded?
Am I unable to bear anything?
Do I allow myself to be unfriendly?
Am I harsh to anyone? Frequently?
Am I bitter to anyone? Constantly?
Do I rejoice at the misfortunes of others?
Do I think of means of revenge? Of getting even?
Am I of an argumentative disposition?
Have I a spirit of contradiction?
Am I given to ridicule of persons, places, or things?
Is my speech sharp, sullen, surly, rude?
Is the tone of my voice such that others think
    I am angry?
Am I sarcastic?
Am I stubborn in disposition?
Do I take sides with those at variance, thus
    increasing the differences?
Do I carry tales?
Do I cause others to be peevish, irritable, impatient, angry?
Do I avoid anyone through anger?
Do I stay angry at others, refusing to speak to them?
Do I readily grant pardon to those who ask for it?
Am I hard to get along with?

What have I done to bring my temper under control?
Have I really made an effort to be even-tempered?
Have I striven to be meek?

It is not necessary to state that one can have a proneness to anger and yet not become angry; practice has brought the temper under control. It is also true that one could be internally angry and yet not give external expression to it by word or conduct, though it is hard to hide anger from being seen. Temptation would have internal anger satisfied by saying something or doing something. Experience shows that there is scarcely any limit to what an angry person may say; angry speech usually goes into angry conduct.

When I feel anger coming on, do I try to stop it?
When I feel angry, do I guard against speaking or acting?
If I become angry, do I allow other ill effects to follow?
Do I carry grudges or remain on the outs with anyone?
Do I speak to such a one coldly?
Do I speak of his faults? Laugh at him? Show signs of
   contempt for him?
Do I criticize him, making him the mark of false humor?
Do I say things to hurt him purposely?
Do I speak and act uncharitably toward him?
Do I act angrily and yet not say anything?

Anger very often rushes to calumny.
Do I accuse my neighbor of faults he has not?
Do I accuse him of sins he has not committed?
Do I misinterpret the words or actions of another?
Do I deny the good actions of another?
Do I deny the good qualities of another?
Do I exaggerate the faults or defects of another?

Rooting Out Hidden Faults

Do I belittle the qualities of another?
Am I silent when another is calumniating?
Do I deny credit to another for what he has done?
Does my anger make me calumniate?

Anger very often rushes to detraction.
Do I talk about the faults of others?
Do I reveal the faults or defects of others?
Do I reveal the faults of others from the wrong motive?
Do I reveal such faults not openly but through hints?
From the way I act, could others guess hidden faults
    of others?
Have I revealed the faults of another by word, or look,
    or sign?
Does my anger make me detract? Backbite?

Anger very often rushes to lying.
Does anger make me lie in a joking way?
Does anger try to make me harm another?
Does anger make me lie for my own benefit? To win an
    argument? A point?
Does anger make me conceal things from one who has a
    right to know?
Does anger make me conceal part of the truth?
Does anger make me exaggerate or belittle?
Does anger make me keep quiet when I should speak?
Does anger make me boast about myself? Another?
    A place? A thing?
Do I say indiscreet things when I am angry?
Does anger make me lie about things?
Does anger make me lie in arguments?
Does lying in an argument make me more angry?

How to Overcome Anger

To overcome temptations to anger, pray perseveringly and fight. Be on guard against it in the morning, and especially at the times or places that were the occasions of falls or temptations in the past. If you happen to fall, rise quickly and with renewed resolution; resolve and resolve and resolve. Learn to hate the sin of anger and all things that give rise to it. Mortify the mind and senses. Never act under the influence of anger.

To overcome anger, practice charity. Pray for the grace of perfect charity; seek occasions to practice charity. Strive to be humble. See the good in everybody; close your eyes to the defects of others; act toward all as you would have all act toward you. Be kind, be patient, envy not, deal not perversely, be not puffed up, rejoice not in iniquity, bear all things, endure all things. Do not allow games to be anything but good fun. Overcome any dislikes, no matter how small. Make a strong effort to be on good terms with everybody; seek to build up a reputation for friendliness.

To overcome anger, practice meekness. Guard meekness by practicing it, by praying for it, by avoiding those sins and imperfections that are opposed to it. Learn to be kind, amiable, friendly, agreeable, pleasant. Preserve evenness of temper. Seek peace of mind, of tongue, of conduct by being gentle, though firm and strong. Love all in Our Lord; love those who are not friendly.

To overcome anger, pray and fight and watch. Renew your resolutions daily. Especially keep in mind the advice of St. Francis de Sales:

> It is a matter of great importance to make our conversation agreeable. To do so it is necessary to appear humble, patient, respectful, cordial, yielding in all lawful things to all. Above all, we must avoid contradicting the opinion

of anyone, unless there is an evident necessity for it. In that case, it should be done with all possible mildness, and with the greatest tact, without in the least outraging the feelings of the other party. In this way we shall avoid contests which produce only bitterness and which ordinarily spring rather from attachment to our own opinion than from love of truth. Believe me, there are no dispositions more inimical to human society than those which are given to contradiction, just as there is not a person more commonly loved than he who contradicts no one.

Chapter 10

∞

Gluttony as a Predominant Fault

Gluttony is an inordinate love of eating and drinking. It is the "eat, drink, and be merry" idea. It is the opposite of "Whether you eat or drink, or whatsoever else you do, do all to the glory of God" (1 Cor. 10:31). Necessity and right reason should regulate our thoughts, words, and acts in regard to eating or drinking. Temperance in eating and drinking is a virtue.

In our day, the tendency is to think and speak much about things to eat and drink. Emphasis is placed on physical fitness. In fact, there are many who practice self-denial for the sake of physical fitness alone. Now, there is no doubt that temperance is a help to health; but should not the spiritual idea come first? Temperance is a virtue; to practice it is to gain merit and grace; to practice it is a means of keeping well.

Right reason should regulate our lives in regard to eating and drinking. We should think correctly in this matter; our state of mind should be spiritual. We eat to live; we should not live to eat. Excess is to be avoided, and so is defect; to be overfed or undernourished is harmful and wrong. Prudence is the guide, for what might be too much or too little for one is not excessive or defective for another. Let reason determine the amount to be taken and the manner in which it is taken.

Yet one could be careful in avoiding what is wrong in regard to quantity and not be mindful of faults arising in regard to quality. We are prone to be particular, not being satisfied with what is served or the way it is served. Things are not at times to our special taste. Inwardly, if not outwardly, we are ready to find fault. And yet our disapproval may be wholly unjustified. What is served is, as a matter of fact, all right, but our taste demands something more delicate or special or particular. Of course, where something special is needed for the sake of health, reason allows it, even though it be frequent or daily.

St. Thomas explains the harmful effects of gluttony. These are: inability to pray or follow a true spiritual standard, foolish joy, frivolity, talkativeness, and temptations against the holy virtue. Any one of these reasons should help us to keep in check our temptations to gluttony; the danger of temptations against the holy virtue should more than suffice for the practice of self-denial.

Ordinarily the person who is inclined to eat or drink to excess is selfish; in other words, selfishness is a sign that one is inclined to gluttony. He shows it by his neglect of the ordinary rules of good breeding; he manifests his thinking of self by searching for the best, by noticing what others take or leave; he neglects the needs of others. He may even go to useless expense to satisfy himself. He will most likely do little to mortify himself, though he does pay attention to the mortifications of others; or if he does at times practice self-denial, he compares what he does with what he thinks or observes others do. Usually he makes a show of his mortifications, congratulating himself while condemning others for what they do. The selfish person thinks of self, takes care of self, is ever ready to eat or drink and willing to talk about either. Thinking of self, he forgets others.

From the following, each one can determine for himself whether gluttony is his predominant fault:

Have I an inordinate love of eating and drinking?

Do I eat or drink to excess?

Do I take what is necessary?

Do I think much about eating and drinking?

Am I critical about the quantity or quality of food served?

Do I compare things with finer things elsewhere?

Do I want better things than those served?

Do I eat or drink hastily? Greedily? Eagerly?

Do I eat or drink things I should not?

Do I waste things?

Am I selfish?

Am I watchful of what another takes?

Do I like to speak about good things to eat or drink?

Do I observe the ordinary rules of politeness?

Do I listen to the reading at table?

Am I fretful or impatient about delays in service?

Do I grumble or complain about the service?

Do I criticize the servers?

Do I practice self-denial? Daily? Frequently? At least in small ways?

Am I prudent about my mortifications?

Have I consistently practiced the virtue of temperance?

How to Overcome Gluttony

To overcome gluttony or any tendency to it, practice mortification. Self-denial is the root of all virtue; there is no worthwhile spiritual life without it. Temperance is a virtue that grows through practice, and temperance demands self-denial. Of course, one should pray to be temperate, for there is no gaining of any virtue except through prayer.

Mortification kills any tendency to gluttony. We can see the necessity of mortification when we consider the evil effects of gluttony. This vice hurries a neglect of religious duties and soon kills fervor and attraction for spiritual things. Necessarily it brings about sloth, languor, and listlessness and consequently prepares the way for temptations against the holy virtue. It also makes serious study impossible. Indulged in to any extent, gluttony brings about proportionate harm, physically, mentally, and spiritually.

Mortification is necessary for the acquiring of any virtue. To practice it for the sake of being temperate would be to receive further fruits, for it keeps the senses under control; it is an aid to recollection and piety; it is a means of increasing in virtue.

Mortification of the senses is necessary. The eyes need to be brought under control; the ears should be regulated; touch ought to be held in subjection; the tongue, as the organ of speech, should be held in check. Not to practice mortification of the senses is not to advance in holiness and is a sure way of falling into many daily faults and even sins.

The sense of taste should be mortified through fasting or abstinence. Some saints fasted a great deal; others at certain but frequent intervals; still others at appointed times. Fasting, of course, should be governed by prudence, and ordinarily permission for it should be sought. Abstinence is something we can all practice daily. We need not abstain from any one thing wholly, but we can deny ourselves in small ways and even at and between meals. Taking less of something, being unselfish, being satisfied with what is placed before us, are reasonable ways of being abstinent.

Corporal mortification should be prudently entered upon and followed; permission should be had. The use of the hair shirt, of the discipline, or chain, or anything that inflicts pain should be a hidden way of practicing virtue.[5] All of the above methods of corporal mortification are useful, helpful, and, for some, necessary. However, what may be useful for one may not be useful for another; what may be helpful for one may not be for another; what may be necessary for one may not be for another. No matter how good one is, no matter how poor one's standard, corporal mortification should be helpful.

Mortification should not be talked about or displayed. One does not hold self up as an example of any other virtue; why this one? The silent influence of virtue is so powerful that it does not need self-praise to give it force or effectiveness. Silly boasting is not fruitful; in fact, it lends itself to ridicule. Those with a false sense of fun will tease or taunt, ask or beg, and may even condemn for lack of comradeship. In our day, there is need of commonsense thinking and speaking about temperance, total abstinence, and mortification, and we who are following the Master should help others to think and speak correctly.

---

[5] Standards of mortification have changed throughout the years, and what damages the health of the body is not encouraged. Nor should corporal mortification be undertaken without the guidance of a superior. However, the idea that any mortification should be kept hidden is the heart of this message and should be kept. —Ed.

Chapter 11

∞

Envy as a Predominant Fault

Envy is the feeling of sadness that we experience in contemplating the prosperity of others, insofar as we regard this prosperity to be our own loss. There is no question that we do have temptations to envy. We are somewhat inclined to rejoice at the failures of others and to be sad at their success. Others achieve riches, honors, dignities, renown, reputation, praise, applause, success; we see what they have accomplished, and we are tempted to envy. Others have qualities of mind and, through their use, become more or less successful, and we are tempted to envy. Others have qualities of soul and reach certain or higher degrees of holiness, and we are tempted to envy. It should be remembered that what those others have we regard as our own loss. It is hard for us to rejoice wholeheartedly at the success of others; it is easy for us to feel glad at their failures.

Envy will try to show itself in some of the following ways:

Do I feel sad at the prosperity of others?

At their success in games? In athletics?

Do I rejoice at their failures?

Do I envy the riches of others?

Do I envy their honors? Dignities? Power? Renown?
Reputation?
Do I envy the applause given to them?
Do I envy another's intellectual qualities?
Do I envy his imagination? Memory? Power of
reasoning? Understanding?
Do I envy his general ability?
Do I envy his learning? His scholarship?
Do I envy another spiritually?
Do I envy his prayerfulness?
Do I envy his rule keeping?
Do I envy his practice of virtue?
Do I envy his obedience? Humility? Mortification?
Love of God?
Do I envy his goodness? His zeal in striving for it?
Does envy make me hate or dislike others?
Does envy make me detract? Calumniate? Find fault?
Does envy make me unfair? Does it make me misjudge?
Misinterpret?
Does envy make me compare myself with others?
Do I try to rejoice at the success of others?
Do I try to be sorry at their failures?
What have I done not to envy in a small way?

How to Overcome Envy

To avoid envy, let us pray. Let us practice self-denial while striving to increase in humility and charity. Let us see the good in everybody. Let us want all to do well. Let us rejoice with others and sorrow with them. Let us realize that we gain nothing by being envious; in fact, we lose merit and grace. Let us thank God for whatever good is done, no matter who does it.

To avoid envy, let us be reasonable. God has given us certain physical, mental, and spiritual talents. He expects us to use them, to increase in them, to bring them back multiplied. He has a place in life for us; He gives us the grace to fill that place; we please Him in accepting His will and following it. What He has allowed others is no concern of ours; they have their duties and obligations. So it is unreasonable and sinful to deplore the gifts of God; it is sinful and unreasonable to deplore what others have, believing that the prosperity of others is our loss. We should live up to our physical, mental, and spiritual talents and be assured that we are doing the will of God.

We should have charity for the manual labor of others. Manual labor is a necessity. The ability brought to it differs; all are not suited to the particular tasks that they are called upon to do. Consequently, what is accomplished will vary according to ability, natural aptitude, or training; sometimes perfect, now more or less imperfect. It is not the perfection of the work alone that counts; it is the spirit in which it was done, the effort with which it was done, the motive used for doing it. Spirit and effort and motive do not imply that any set work should therefore be perfect. Yet how quick we sometimes are to accept complainingly what another has done, especially when it affects us in any way. Looking at how it could have been done, and perhaps better done, we fail to give the due credit by refusing to see the spirit behind it all, the effort put forth, and the motive governing it. When another is allowed to do what we wanted to do, envy comes along to tempt us, trying to make us feel sad if that work is done well, or trying to make us rejoice if it is done poorly. We can be so uncharitable in this regard.

Charity should also cover recreation. Games give rise to mechanical or mental mistakes. Because we are not perfect, we make mistakes that are involuntary, mistakes into which we did not want to fall and which we did all in our power to avoid. Training and a reasonable amount of carefulness should help us not to commit the same errors time after time; effort should help us to avoid them; commonsense thinking should be of assistance. Still, in spite of training and effort and thinking, we can make mistakes. Charity, ordinary kindness, forbids us to find fault or criticize or condemn him who does what he cannot help, whether such is due to lack of ability, a learning of the game, or a lack of aptitude in playing the particular game in question.

What applies to mechanical mistakes also concerns errors of judgment. Mental mistakes prove that we are human and therefore not perfect; anyone is liable to forget or do the wrong thing under stress. Surely we understand that. Who tries to do the wrong thing? Consequently, there is need of patience, meekness, kindness, charity. Moreover, we should remember that not only as beginners did we fall into mistakes, but even at the time when we considered ourselves as quite adept.

Spectators should be charitable. We are prone to take sides, to favor one rather than another. We are really never strictly neutral. Though we are not actually playing the game, we can play it in an offensive way. We can forget the consideration that is due to losers; we can think merely of the winners and, for that reason, can descend into ridicule, insult, or unsportsmanlike remarks or conduct. Moreover, we can envy the success of those we oppose or rejoice at their failure. If we are actually playing a game, we should be on our guard not to allow our own interests to lead us to faults or sins of envy. Charity is the virtue of recreation.

There should be charity for the spiritual standards of others. He who is ready to find fault with the standards of another had better look to his own, for the critical viewpoint must pull down.

He who would criticize another's goodness is thereby proclaiming how poor is his own goodness. The first concern of each one should be his own duties in regard to prayer, to rule keeping, to obedience, to mortification, to humility, to any virtue; and no matter how good he is, he does not make his second concern the spiritual lives of others—except to help. To speak about others in a critical way is to fall. We should have sympathy for the weak; advice, if it will be heeded; prayer for all, that God may foster more perfect service.

God wants saints; God desires perfection. Piety should be held in high esteem; so should rule keeping, obedience, mortification, and every other virtue. It is a woefully sad state of affairs when anyone is ridiculed for his goodness. It would be a deplorable condition if we tried to keep anyone from becoming holy. It would be even worse to endeavor to pull one down from a high standard that he has acquired. Envy wants failure. There are those who have kept others from being good; and there are those who sneered at another's goodness, so that he fell; there are those who have willfully and deliberately tempted others by trying to make them disobey, or lie, or cheat, or give up their mortifications, and so forth. Do we bear any guilt in this matter?

There should be charity for the intellectual life of others. Give credit to those to whom it is due. Praise those who excel. Be sympathetically kind to those who are not doing well. Be considerate of those who make mistakes. We should want what every teacher desires—a perfect standard on the part of each member of a class. Let us be fair and just in what we think and say about the intellectual life of others. Let not their success be our sorrow; nor their failures, our joy. Envy not, but be charitable.

Fr. Faber gives the following rules for the practice of fraternal charity:

Rooting Out Hidden Faults

1. Often reflect on some good point in each of your brethren.
2. Reflect on the opposite faults in yourself.
3. Do this most in the case of those whom you are most inclined to criticize.
4. Never claim rights, or even let ourselves feel that we have them, as this spirit is most fatal to obedience and charity.
5. Charitable thoughts are the only security for charitable deeds and words. They save us from surprises, especially from surprises of temper.
6. Never have an aversion for another, much less manifest it.
7. Avoid particular friendships.
8. Never judge another. Always, if possible, excuse the faults we see, and if we cannot excuse the action, excuse the intention. We cannot all think alike, and we should, therefore, avoid attributing bad motives to others.

Let us be loyal to the community within and without. Certainly it is sufficiently harmful to criticize within the community. Yet we can forget our duty here. There is no excuse for him who carries his criticisms to outsiders. Charity is a community virtue. We are following the Master. We are gathered for His work. He has employed us in a special way. He wants us to have His spirit. So He asks us not only to have that charity that is due to all but also that special charity for those who follow Him. Family spirit demands it; the effective work of any group of associates depends on it.

Charity should kill self-love, self-will. The tendency is to think of self as the large interest. Consideration for others is second in thought, and for the very reason that we have such a proneness, we are ready to forget that self should not be the only consideration. Self-will wants to go its own way; self-love desires to follow that which is pleasing to it. Virtue is forgetfulness of self. Virtue thinks of God and one's neighbor through God.

To be charitable, we must learn to think charitably. It is no easy matter to keep our thoughts in check. Sometimes we are indisposed, things did not go so as to suit us, we did not have our own way in regard to something, we had opposition, we had difficulties, and thus the temptation to think uncharitably. Moreover, our very zeal, our interest, our wholehearted endeavor can lead us to uncharitableness, for we can become discontented when our zeal and interest and endeavor are not followed by others or not given due credit by them.

It is something, and a great something, to think charitably; it is still more to speak charitably. Who is there that has not been involuntarily uncharitable in speech? We did not give sufficient reflection to what we were about to say; we used tones of voice that were sharp. This indeliberate uncharitableness arises especially in argument, in explanations, in self-defense, in innocent fun at another's expense, bits of irony or sarcasm or ridicule. Should we not try to avoid even indeliberate uncharitableness?

We should learn to be charitable in conduct. We are all tempted to offend this way; and as a matter of fact, because we are not always the same, not always cheerful, or pleasant, or meek, but sometimes serious or out of sorts, we do offend. Our changes of mood react on others. They notice them; they wonder what is wrong; they are attracted or repelled by the way we act. Even temper is well worth acquiring. To be the same: amiable, pleasant, agreeable, patient, meek, mild, sociable, obliging—to be ever the same toward others is to practice charity in a high manner. If our mood changes at all, let it be something more in charity; let us "be all in all to all"; let our standard constantly ascend. Let our charity become habitual.

Chapter 12

Sloth as a Predominant Fault

Sloth is an inordinate love of rest, which leads us to omit or neglect our duties. Physical, mental, and spiritual duties are before us daily; sloth tries to enter into them.

The parable of the call of the laborers to the vineyard is worthy of consideration when we speak about sloth. It will be recalled that Our Lord likens the Kingdom of Heaven to the householder who hired men: some of them early in the morning, others at the third or sixth hour, and still others at the eleventh hour. And Our Lord, in calling men to His kingdom, is ever on the alert, even to the end of the day. He wants to be the Master, the employer, of all men; He desires the service of all; He yearns for it; He died for all. All men should work for Him; sloth refuses wholly or in part.

God is persistently calling men to His vineyard. Many answer the call; they work for a while; they serve God; then they cease to labor; evidently they stop thinking about the end of day and the pay that has been offered. They are prodigals. Sin and perhaps continued sin and failure to employ grace and the sacraments place them among the idle, among those who walk away from Him and into the paths of adversity. Still God continues to call them; He wants them to come back and take up their work for Him; He asks them to be sorry for having quit; He asks them to begin all over.

Others also has God called to His vineyard. They begin to work for Him; they labor in faithful service, though at times they fall into sin. Undoubtedly they are far from perfection in their work, but they realize their weaknesses through remorse of conscience, and they take up their tasks with new heart and new resolution. They are good in the eyes of God in spite of their frailties. God wants them to continue to serve Him, for He knows and they understand that future and even present happiness lies in such employment. Such souls, nearly always faithful, go through life making false steps and never reaching holiness, but nevertheless working for Him who rewards those who have served Him and die holily in His service.

There are others in the vineyard who are almost saints. They are so close to perfection that the wonder is that they don't fight sloth and work with a little more zeal to reach holiness. If they were only a little better, they would be saints, though hidden saints. They love the Church; they glory in the Church. They love the Master, and they are eager and anxious to work for Him, believing all the time that what they do is incomparably small next to what He has done for them. How they serve God with that faith! What glory to the Church such souls are! What sources of edification they are to others!

There are saints in the vineyard. Look at the history of the saints, and you will notice that some never left the work of God for sin; sloth could not draw them down. They were holy all the days of their lives, growing more perfect and closer to God the longer they lived and, consequently, the longer they served. Their perseverance in the zealous labor never wavered; in fact, it constantly increased. What tabernacles such souls must have been! A thousand acts each day made them more lovely; a thousand unreckoned graces made them more beautiful. God was ever present to add to their wonderfulness. Such holiness is answering God's call to labor for Him without reservation, without any thought but doing all for Him. Such holiness is continued loving service. And what think you will be the reward?

There are other saints in the vineyard. These were called at the third or sixth or eleventh hour. When their call came, they were ready to turn to holy work for Him. They did not question the lateness of the hour or worry about the reward. Their day of conversion was at hand, and they answered unreservedly. Once they had begun, they did not turn back. They set their minds and their hearts on holiness, and they reached it with persevering zeal. The work may have been hard; they had difficulties, and, more than likely, trying difficulties; but they were big and brave enough to throw aside the temptations that would seek to hold them back.

Has not a spark of grace fired your soul, so that you resolved and renewed your resolution to give perfect service to God? Were you afraid to try to be holy? Did temptation make you believe that you had started so late or had so much to do that there was no use working at all? What is there to stop you from beginning right now to work perfectly for God? Your resolution with God's grace can lead to great heights. Perhaps not to the mountain of holiness that the saints reached, but nevertheless to great spirituality. St. Francis of Assisi began late; so did Magdalene; so did Augustine; and the Good Thief very late. But it is a question of when you begin. It is not too late to start now; but it will be too late after a while, for to have such a thought is to plan not to answer the call to work.

Rooting Out Hidden Faults

Consider all the daily means to advance in holiness; think of all the graces at your command; what opportunities! Have you not seen others reach up to what they have? Will you try?

The lesson of the parable does not only refer to spiritual things as such. Laboring for the Master includes manual labor, recreation, studies. God wants us to serve Him faithfully in each of these, giving Him as perfect a service as possible. Could we not raise our standard in our studies? Could we not increase in our spirit of study and perseveringly be faithful to it? Could we not show more attention, more application, more willingness to learn? Could we not elevate our standard in recreation? In any work that we are called upon to do? A little more effort, a little more zeal, a little less sloth, and we would be rendering to God the service that He wants, that He has actually called us to, and for which He will reward us.

Too many persons are satisfied with mediocrity. They are neither good nor bad; they are ordinary, commonplace; and they remain so through their own fault. Let us glance over the various kinds of mediocrity and then determine whether or not we are ordinary. Some are mediocre in general. They have a lukewarm, careless attitude about everything. Their standard is ordinary in regard to spiritual things, to studies, to manual labor, to the proper attitude in recreation. They do not pray well or keep rules; they do not study with any real effort; they work in an indifferent way; they are slothful even in games. There are others who are lukewarm concerning some particular thing: they are ordinary in spiritual affairs, or studies, or manual labor, or recreation. Certain others are mediocre in a still more particular way: they practice obedience, or charity, or mortification, or rule keeping in an ordinary way. They have a pronounced weakness, and seemingly sloth holds them in power, for they do not correct what is at fault; and the danger is that this one weakness will spread and become the cause of other falls. Those who are mediocre as far as studies are concerned have commonplace attention, or application, or effort, or willingness to learn. It may be they have a class to which they give no interest or very little; or they are neglecting a certain study that is hard for them. Those who are mediocre in regard to manual labor work in a careless or lazy fashion, being satisfied with indifferent results. Those who are mediocre in recreation commit the same faults time after time; they do not urge themselves to better things; they lack zeal in the correction of their faults; they remain uncharitable.

Now, none of us would care to be mediocre in everything, but are there not any number of us who seem to be satisfied with mediocrity in a particular way? Sloth keeps us from perfection; sloth holds us back; sloth enters daily into some of the things we do.

Sloth tries to enter into spiritual affairs.

Am I slothful?

Have I an inordinate love of rest, neglecting my duties?

Have I an attraction for spiritual things?

Do I make resolutions and try to keep them?

Do I pray with fervor, with piety? Is my attention fixed
on the words or their meaning? On God?

Do I offer lip service?

Am I lukewarm? Indifferent? Careless?

Do I pray as a mere matter of routine?

Do I allow distractions to remain?

Am I mediocre at prayer?

Do I practice recollection?

Do I make sufficient effort?

Rooting Out Hidden Faults

Do I tire easily when praying?

Do I go through exercises half-heartedly?

Do I hurry through my prayers?

Do I complain about the length of prayers? Exercises?

Do I rush on leaving exercises?

Do I assist at prayers in a lazy posture?

Do I genuflect reverently?

Do I make the Sign of the Cross reverently?

Do I observe the rubrics in serving Mass? Assisting at Mass?

Do I have respect for sacred places, persons, and things?

Do I have confidence, humility, perseverance, fervor in my prayers?

What have I done to improve my standard in prayers?

Have I made an effort to get rid of my faults — especially my predominant fault?

Is my obedience prompt, entire, cheerful, supernatural?

Do I mortify my mind and my senses?

Have I grown more humble?

Do I hate sin and try to avoid it?

Am I meek, patient, kind, obliging?

Am I modest?

Do I love God because He has been good to me? Above all things?

Do I love God for Himself alone?

Is there any virtue in which I am mediocre?

Do I commit venial sins?

Do I fall into deliberate imperfections? What about my rule keeping?

Do I want to be perfect?

Have I perseveringly tried to improve?

Sloth tries to enter into mental affairs.

Am I slothful in regard to studies?

Do I make an effort to study?

Do I waste time?

Do I allow distractions to remain?

Do I grow tired easily?

Do I seek excuses to get out of studying or
the work assigned?

Do I get merely the work assigned? Or is it my
best effort?

Do I copy or cheat on a quiz or examination?

Am I careless? Indifferent?

Do I try to make my work neat? Correct? Accurate?

Do I neglect any class?

Do I realize that perfect silence helps me study?

Am I diligent in the preparation of my classes?

Do I control my eyes? Ears? Tongue?

What is my standard in class?

Do I lack diligence?

Do I lack attention?

Am I willing to learn?

Am I obedient?

Am I humble about my talents, work, answers, conduct?

Do I keep silence? Do I prompt others? Make signs? Pass
notes?

Am I guilty of frivolity?

Do I ask questions without thinking?

Do I put too much time on one class, neglecting
others?

What zeal have I used to acquire a spirit of study?

Do I try to be faithful to my studies?

Sloth tries to show itself in deed.

Do I act lazily?

Am I too fond of rest?

Do I take lazy positions in answering prayers?

Do I kneel in a lounging way?

Do I walk in a lazy way?

Am I too deliberate in the way I do things?

Do I act promptly, wholeheartedly, cheerfully, supernaturally?

Do I do things poorly, sluggishly, remissly?

Am I changeable? Fickle? Tiring of something quickly?

Do I delight in idle conversation?

Have I a lazy way of speaking?

Do I dress slovenly?

Do I choose the company of those who are not doing well?

What is my standard in recreation?

Is my conduct sportsmanlike?

Am I careless about modesty, charity, truthfulness?

Am I indifferent to a standard that is honest, just, fair?

Am I mediocre about meekness?

Is there any virtue that I practice in a mediocre way in recreation?

What have I done not to be slothful in deed?

Could I do more?

How to Overcome Sloth

Do we do all to please God? Is this our motive for manual labor? If it is, we work promptly, cheerfully, wholeheartedly; we plan our work and do it orderly; there is nothing slipshod about it;

there is nothing, be it ever so slight, that is willfully left undone; we do a finished bit of work.

Zeal in studies can be acquired. Zeal demands attention. Attention grows through practice; so does application. And these ordinarily foster a desire to learn. Now as never before, the world needs learned, intellectual leaders who are guided by Catholic principles. Therefore, we who are following a vocation should use every opportunity to acquire a true spirit of study, for the more mentally developed we are, the greater will be our work for God.

Zeal in spiritual affairs can be acquired. Tepidity can be overcome by persevering effort. Perfection should be our goal, even though we never reach it. To try to keep rules perfectly is soon to love to keep rules; to labor to be free from venial sin is quickly to be working against imperfection; to acquire virtue is to set the mind on the important virtues—humility, mortification, piety, obedience, love of neighbor and God—practicing them daily. To be attentive in prayer, then, be faithful in getting rid of distractions that arise in the making of the regular exercises. To be fervent, keep trying to be fervent. Have confidence in persevering prayer.

Do not lose heart in fighting against sloth. Repeat your resolutions frequently during the day. Prayer and effort are the means to success. We are not working alone: God's grace is with us, if we ask for it. Let us ask for it perseveringly.

Chapter 13

∞

Atonement

Wound of the Left Foot

Let us beg pardon for our sins.

O my God, I repent from the bottom of my heart
for having offended Thee, who are infinitely good. I
embrace the feet of Thy Son and beseech Thee, by the
wound of His left foot, to vouchsafe to say to me, as He
did to Magdalene: "Thy sins are forgiven thee."

We should make acts of sorrow for our sins and imperfections.
We have sinned, and we have been guilty of imperfection, and
we should be sorry — not with a sorrow that worries or frets,
but with a sorrow that is more and more a realization that we
have offended God; not with a sorrow that says we have done
wrong, but with a sorrow that states we have offended God by
such wrong.

Our sorrow at Particular Examen should concern our falls
into our predominant fault, our failure to practice the virtue
opposed to our predominant fault, our forgetfulness to practice
our strongest virtue, our carelessness in practicing the presence

of God. Let our acts of sorrow arise from our heart and in our own words.

ACTS OF SORROW

O my God, I am heartily sorry for having offended Thee, because Thou art infinitely good and amiable, and because sin displeases Thee. I am firmly resolved, with the help of Thy grace, to do penance for my sins and never to offend Thee again.

O Mary, refuge of sinners, obtain for me the grace to efface from my soul the title of sinner. O Mother of God, pray for a poor sinner who places all his confidence in thee.

O my God, I am sorry for having offended Thee. I regret that I have allowed my predominant fault to overcome me. I am sorry that I have done so little in acquiring virtue. May my sorrow increase and help me never to offend Thee again.

Venial sin offends God. "Who would dare affirm," asks St. Anselm, "that a sin is not a great evil because it is light? How can we call light an evil that dishonors God?" Venial sin offends God; and in a lesser way, imperfection offends God. Should not that arouse our sorrow? Deliberately and willfully shall we continue to offer offense, insult? Would we dare to offend another daily and day after day? Shall we allow ourselves to become so hardened in light sins as to make little or nothing of them? Shall we tire God with our small offenses and at the same time refuse to accept the grace that He is offering? Shall we make so little of His friendship as to be willing to lose it altogether?

God is calling us to perfection; He asks us to live our vocation. "Be ye perfect" demands persevering effort, though perfection itself is not reached. "Be ye perfect" consists in steady zeal in striving for holiness. It would be absurd to think of making great progress if numerous venial sins are being committed, for there is no question that such sins weaken the powers of the soul, making the will unsteady and irresolute, while preparing the way to serious sin. Numerous venial sins, made little of, eventually lead to mortal sin. Imperfections check progress and make ready the path to venial sin.

Now, it is true that we cannot hope to overcome all deliberate sins and imperfections. Nevertheless, even here we can make progress by not falling into deliberate sins and imperfections. The greater our control over deliberate wrong, the greater our control over indeliberate wrong.

To make our acts of sorrow at Particular Examen efficacious, we can impose slight penances on ourselves. We must make satisfaction for all our sins and imperfections, so what better time or method than daily small penances, self-inflicted? All things can be used to pay our debt of punishment: our keeping of rules; accepted humiliations; bits of mortification; acts of meekness, patience, charity; the practice of any virtue; the saying of prayers, especially prayers of sorrow.

All acts of sorrow demand a purpose of amendment, a resolution made here and now not to offend God again. This purpose of amendment should be personal, something that fits our daily life; it should be practical, something in particular to be done or avoided; it should be for the day at hand, not made for tomorrow or some future day. When our resolutions are personal and practical and for the day at hand, we can with God's grace carry them out more easily.

Chapter 14

~

Resolution

Wound of the Heart of Jesus

Let us renew our morning resolutions.

O Jesus! O God of love; from this time forth, I will satisfy
the just desires of Thy Heart, pierced on the Cross for
my salvation, and correct all my sins and negligences.
Confirm me in these resolutions and in those of my
morning meditation, through the merits of the Blood
that flowed for me from Thy Heart; I offer them to Thee
in atonement with Thy life, Thy Passion, and Thy death.

Resolutions are necessary if we wish to make progress. We need
grace to make and keep them. Let us ask for that grace in our
own words. We can use the following prayers,

PRAYERS FOR HELP TO KEEP RESOLUTIONS

O good Jesus, we humbly ask Thee to help us keep our
resolutions, so that, under Thy protection, we may not
want the fervent effort that is necessary to follow Thee
perfectly.

Grant, we beseech Thee, O Lord, the grace that will keep us constantly strong in following our resolutions, that through them we may draw closer and closer to Thee.

May Thy grace, O Lord, always accompany us and assist us in the pious accomplishment of the resolutions that Thou hast inspired, so that we may serve Thee perfectly.

It is not always easy to make suitable resolutions at meditation. Consequently, there should be other daily resolutions. There are many from which to choose. Undoubtedly our first determination should concern our motive: do all to please God. When the saints followed their vocation, they answered unreservedly; they acted generously. When they responded, there was no holding back of their minds or senses. They were determined to give all to the Master; they were resolved to do all for Him. Whatever would make them draw closer to God, they did. Not only did they want to be considered faithful, but they also worked to be perfect; they tried to do all for God as perfectly as they could. They conformed their thoughts and words and deeds to those of God; they saw His will in everything, and they sought to do it.

To do all for God means that we should resolve to avoid sin and imperfection. God's grace is ready to help, if we are willing to make the effort necessary to be faithful to it. Surely we should be concerned about our salvation and holiness. Let our zeal grow in avoiding venial sin; let our effort be more constant in keeping rules; let us not tire in avoiding evil and doing good; let us persevere in our determination, though there be difficulties. Certainly, in working for God we should be courageous enough and generous enough to do His will even though it means a cross.

Let us, then, strive to live perfect days—days in which we have committed no deliberate sin and no deliberate imperfection. Let us try so to live as to go to Confession with no sins or imperfections to confess.

We should resolve to practice the important virtues—love of God and neighbor, obedience, mortification, humility, piety. Could not our obedience be more prompt, more cheerful, more wholehearted, more truly supernatural? Could not our humility be more of a doing all for God, nothing for self and nothing for the glory of fellow men? Could not our mortification of mind and senses be more perfect? Could we not increase our piety by being more attentive at prayer? Could we not have a truer charity for those about us? Could not our love of God be more entire and generous? Surely there is something we can do to make the practice of these virtues show that we sincerely mean to do all to please God.

We should resolve to make our studies spiritual. The right motive is necessary. With the motive to do all to please God we should aim to acquire a spirit of application, a spirit of attention, a spirit of silence, a desire to learn, and perseverance. Study and class standards should be as high as we can make them. Perfection is the goal, even though we fall short of it. Let us seek learning, culture, scholarship, character by faithfulness to our daily work.

We should make our recreation spiritual. We should practice charity and meekness, honesty, truthfulness, good sportsmanship, modesty. These virtues imply consideration for others and urge us to think of their happiness. We should resolve to keep our standard high and do nothing that would lower the standards of others.

We must pray to be faithful to our resolutions. We are not working alone; God is with us. He helps us with His grace. We may not, and undoubtedly will not, be as perfect as we should be; we may not keep our resolutions perfectly, but we can renew them and renew them, thereby showing that we are not weak-hearted or lacking in courage. Let a spiritual discontent seize us; let it make us dissatisfied with ourselves; let it ever urge us on to higher and better things; let our "pray hard and study hard and play hard" grow in meaning and let us follow the inspiration of that new meaning. Let us pray and pray hard to keep our resolutions.

Chapter 15

∞

Faith

There is no fact so glorious as the spread and triumph of the Faith over the world. For three years, Christ had given His message to men. He labored zealously; He kept His purpose in life before Him. He preached truth—the truth that He was the Son of God. He used the prophets, His life, His miracles to prove that His mission was divine. Yet, in spite of His extraordinary goodness, in spite of all His proofs and statements, in spite of all that He had done to show that He came from the Father, He was put to death. Seemingly He had failed. Then, lo and behold, just when His enemies were rejoicing at His death and failure, and His disciples were sorrowing at His horrible ending, He comes to life again. His followers take on new interest and abound with heartfelt willingness to carry on His mission, while His enemies are at a loss as to what to do, except to persecute His disciples. But the very persecution drives the apostles to further conquest, and before they meet death for the Master, they have gone very far and wide; and He whose reign seemed to have ended with the Cross is only begun. What is still more surprising, the most scheming of all the persecutors turns to follow Him whom he tried not to believe in. St. Paul espouses Christianity with a zeal that meant many converts.

The spread of the Faith by the apostles is wonderful in its broadness and quickness. And even after they are gone, the Faith continues to go forth to the world. When the apostles were put to death, it was believed that the Christian Faith would die. Instead, it grew; it increased. Persecutions were zealously carried on throughout the length and breadth of the Roman Empire. All the means of torture that could be devised were used in the vicious purpose to rid the world of Christianity. Persecution followed persecution; thousands perished in those three centuries of terror. Christianity seemed destroyed. Nevertheless, when the Edict of Milan was signed in 313, and religious peace was proclaimed to the world, it was discovered that the Faith was more prosperous than ever. Christ had risen again. The Church was not only not dead, but flourishing.

But peace was hardly proclaimed when the Church had again to suffer for being the bearer of truth. This time she would surely be crushed, for her enemy was an enemy that had left nothing but destruction in its wake. Peace to practice the Faith was to be taken away by this all-absorbing victor. No Church could withstand those barbarous tribes from the North or West. They who dared to defy Caesar could and would take care of this new religion. The country is overrun by barbarians. The Church must die under such oppression. But the savage hordes meet that something that will mean their subjection. When the land is made desolate, when the Master is fled, when the flock is scattered, the Church awakens to another day, and the barbarians have become members of her society, have been civilized. They see the beauty of the Church of God; she appeals to them as she had appealed to other thousands; they have that longing in their hearts for just the things she can give; she is rich with the something that would make this life worthwhile and the next all happiness. They are willing; they are ready; they ask to enter the Church. They, instead of lessening the numbers of the Church, actually add to those numbers by their conversion.

So the Church has gone through the ages. There will always be those who will declare that the Church is dead or dying. There will be those who will rejoice at her apparent failures; there will be those who will offer their help to bury her. Persecutions may come and go, but Christ goes on forever. No one can take away the power of Faith. It will grow and flourish till time is no more. Persecutions, as the ages make manifest, do not destroy or weaken the Church; they give her the opportunity of a glorious and new resurrection. And each individual resurrection proves how steady is her growth and how she continues to increase in numbers.

The spread of the Church is a triumph, and the growth of the Church has meant a growth in the acceptance of her truths. She has given to the world what she has received from Christ and God—moral principles. She has taught God to man. She has demanded from man his duties to God, to himself, and to his fellow men. She has stood before all for God. She has spoken with authority to rulers and ruled, to rich and poor. She has taught the Faith.

It is worthwhile to think of what the Church has done for the world. Remember that she has been the great civilizer. Bear in mind that she has been a leader of culture, that education has always been dear to her; not an education that is satisfied with a mere training of the mind, but a development that has the welfare of the soul at heart. She has thought of the morality of the world in all phases of life. She has taught that all things must be pervaded with the thought that there is a God, who has dominion over all things.

Though the conquest of the world through the gospel has been a glorious triumph, nevertheless it must not be forgotten that the victory was attained by reaching the individual soul. There have been no conversions in large numbers unless the individual has been brought into the Church through Faith. And has not change of life, the conquest of the individual, been the steady aim of the Church? What points more to truth than conversions? Even more than that: What is a more certain sign of the divinity of the Church than the change of a sinner from sin to goodness? Here is one who walks in ways that are defiled, who has tasted and known that sin is a bitter thing, who has lived in sin perhaps for years, who accepts grace leading to conversion, and then begins a life of fidelity to God. To watch the progress of such a soul is to see the fruit of the Church's mission in developing those with Faith. Where once was unfaithfulness and sin is now the constant effort to grow in virtue. Duties to God are not only sought after, but they are also zealously taken up. The former sinner is not satisfied except in doing the will of God.

Yet the conversion of a sinner to ordinary goodness is not so great a triumph for the Faith as is the conversion of a great sinner to great sanctity. Magdalene is praised before the world for giving her whole heart and soul to God. In such a soul, as in the soul of an Augustine, or (in another way) in the soul of a Saul, there was much that had to be eradicated. In the souls of great sinners, there is proneness to sin, a proneness arising from long habits. Such habits are deep-rooted. To change from ordinary goodness would be sufficiently hard, but to change from badness to extraordinary holiness shows the spell that attracts the mind that is willing to see the truth of the Church. To follow such truths is to practice virtue as eagerly as sin had been followed in olden days. To seek to be like the ideal Founder is to have and hold all things as means to perfection. The Church can offer all the means of holiness; the Church can show the way; the Church can say what the means are and how they should be used. The grace to be constant and persevering in following holiness comes from God.

Though we do marvel at the conversion of anyone from a life of sin to a life of holiness, still we must not think of public saints alone. The Church also has her hidden saints. They go on in daily life, doing well what duty imposes on them by urging themselves to higher things and things not imposed by duty. Mere faithfulness to what is commanded is not enough for such souls. They have a desire to give all to God. They offer all to God and perform all as befits such an intention. They are heroic in giving to God all that they can from day to day; they are heroic in their zealous fidelity to what they must do. Certainly they are not satisfied with ordinary, mediocre goodness. Slight sins and even imperfections for them are hateful and as much to be avoided as the more serious offenses. They actually live without falling into faults, at least deliberate. And as they grow from virtue to virtue, they manifest internal goodness in their external conduct. Their motive to do all to please God is ever before them; their obedience — prompt, cheerful, wholehearted, supernatural — shines as a light at night; mortification of the mind and senses is their means of killing self in order that they may live for God; their humility is ever on the increase; they love God and therefore their neighbors; and, in loving both, they take pains not to offer the slightest offense to either. Such love should and does reveal itself in prayer. They are devout. They make the whole day a prayer; they live in the presence of God as far as they can in following their other duties. They have real interest in talking to God. They think of God throughout the day and act according to that thought.

Hidden saints are surely the glory of the Church. Nevertheless, the Church also has her public saints, those whose names are enrolled on the calendar of the Blessed. They stand before the throne of God. They are with Him forever. There will be others who will come to live with them. Without doubt, there are saints living now. And the very striking fact is that even those outside the Church testify to the holiness of those whom the Church has declared or is about to declare holy.

Faith is a precious gift.

Have we valued it properly?

Does it mean more to us than anything else in life?

Have we guarded it and defended it? Have we loved it so
    much that we would be willing to suffer or die for it?

Has it increased?

Do we know more about it?

Do we understand it more fully?

Have we a keener realization of the truths it brings us?

Have we lived it?

Are we faithful to grace and the duties of our state of life?

Do we try to be more and more faithful to our vocation?

Chapter 16

∞

Hope

Hope is a supernatural virtue by which we firmly trust that God will give us everlasting life and the means to obtain it, because He is faithful to His promises.

We are not for this world. We come from God; we belong to God; we are destined for God. When we realize through life's fleeting day that all things are to be measured by the life to come, that material success, honors, riches, and good times mean nothing if they carry us away from our true end, then we live so that we may be found worthy of eternal life. We can forget the Word of God: "What shall it profit a man, if he gain the whole world, and suffer the loss of his soul?" (Mark 8:36). We can stray into a love of this life; luxuries, comforts, and ease are ours to use or abuse; we can be stamped with worldliness. Not that we forget altogether the necessity of saving our souls; no, not that, but we can allow ourselves to become neglectful in the service of God; we can forget to work wholly for Him and the reward He offers—eternal life.

We who are following a vocation are called to a perfection that is not demanded of those in the world. We have our vows as helps; we have more opportunities for doing good; our very duties are so ordered as to aid us to be holy. Do we use what is at our disposal as means of perfection? Do we strive for holiness? We can fail. We can be presumptuous; we can be satisfied with self in spite of the fact that we do not know whether we are "worthy of love or hatred." We can be so concerned with our work, our duties, our helping others to be saved as to run the risk of being castaways. St. Paul saw the danger for himself of being presumptuous: "I chastise my body, and bring it into subjection: lest perhaps, when I have preached to others, I myself should become a castaway" (1 Cor. 9:27). We should meditate on that thought.

Yet there is never reason for despair. God wills us to be saved. We want happiness; that means we want God, for happiness comes from drawing closer to God, not in growing away from Him. Not only does God will us to be saved, but He also gives us the means of salvation, for He is a God of mercy. Men have understood that God is a God of mercy: "From Genesis to the Apocalypse there is heard like the wail of the wind, and the sob of the sea, the cry of stricken humanity pleading with God."[6] Generations were gathered, people strayed from God and tasted of sin, yet He was a Father of mercy. Read the story of the infidelity of the Chosen People; it is one of sins forgiven. Read the history of God's holy nation, of its great leaders, kings, and warriors; it is a record of mercy. "Have mercy on me, O God, according to thy great mercy ... [for] my sin is always before me" (Ps. 50: 3, 5 [51:1, 3]) is a cry that could have been uttered in the Garden after the first sin; it could have been sounded through the early

---

[6] Venerable Fulton Sheen, "The Death of Life," March 5, 1933, CatholicSaints.Info, http://catholicsaints.info/tag/published -in-1933/.

centuries, just as, from David's time, it ascended to the infinite God, till the Master of mercy came.

The Gospel story is one of mercy. There are those who find it hard to live right, for their daily life is spent near sin's seducing influence, or perhaps their lives have been filled with neglect of the ordinary duties of religion. They find it hard to cry to God with a voice of supplication. Old ways are easy; new ways are difficult; it is not easy to ask for mercy. Read the Gospel story. Recall how, a short time before His death, Our Lord wept over apostate, unfaithful, sinful Jerusalem. "Jerusalem, how often I would have taken thee"; oh, the days of unremitting toil, the nights of wasted sleep, the burning tears and feverish thoughts. "Jerusalem, how often I would have gathered together thy children," to keep them, to protect them, to forgive them their sins, to bring them to the Father. "But thou wouldst not" (see Matt. 23:37; Luke 13:34). Yet, in a few days, His life would be offered for those who refused as well as for those who accepted His mercy. In a few days, He would be saying: "Father, forgive them!" (Luke 23:34). There is never any reason to despair. God wants us to come to Him, no matter how unfaithful we have been; He wants us to return home, no matter how far we have been away; He wants us to ask for forgiveness, for He wants us to be saved.

He also asks us to use His grace and be holy. Not only is He willing to give us the means to be saved, but He also offers us the helps to sanctity. Our start may be late; we may have much to do; effort and persevering effort may be trying; still we must remember that when *the* day of conversion has come, we should not harden our hearts. The Master may not pass this way again. The lateness of the hour, the amount to be accomplished, the effort necessary, should not be used as excuses or reasons for not beginning when the soul has been awakened to the thought of a better life. True, there may be temptations that will seek to hold us back; we may even fall; our resolutions may be broken; but can we not take heart again? The struggle will not last forever; it continues until we have rooted out or almost destroyed our bad habits. Not to start at all is to be weak; discouragement is cowardly.

Discontent with self and discouragement are not the same. To be dissatisfied with self is a grace that is part of sorrow; it makes us want to do better, urging us to serve God more faithfully. We have new thoughts about goodness, we see what can be done, we understand the goal to be reached, and we strive, painfully, to reach it, for we do not care to remain where we are. Onward and upward, perfection ever calling, effort ever constant, goodness more and more attractive, new hopes and new ideas, service increasingly wholehearted — blessed fruits of discontent with self.

Temptations may come. Our way may be that of the cross, with sorrow and trials and pain. All these we must gladly employ as a means to do something for God. They give new strength and new purpose; they reveal steadiness of resolution. "To suffer or to die." Faith is kept in spite of adversities; these, in fact, create opportunities for further faithfulness. We rejoice in being able to do something for God; we live to work for Him; we do not ask that the way be made easy, but that we may have a steady purpose and effort, even if the way is hard. We carry our cross joyfully; we live in hope for the good things to come, where "death shall be no more, nor mourning, nor crying" (Rev. 21:4), but instead, happiness with God and His angels and saints.

We learn more and more to resign ourselves to God. We see Him all about us. We trust Him. We have confidence in Him. We know He will be faithful to His word. So when we pray, we pray with humility, realizing our weaknesses and relying on His strength. When we pray, we pray with confidence. We have no fear of denial, for we place our thoughts and prayers before Him, asking Him to do as He wills. We pray with perseverance. We never lose heart. We never grow tired or tepid; we never stop; we even wear away the steps of His altar, for we know, in "a very little while, and he that is to come, will come, and will not delay" (Heb. 10:37).

We are on the road to eternity. Temptations try to take us on devious paths. Spiritual difficulties in studies, work, and temporal affairs would have us go astray. Sin endeavors to attract us. Shall we continue on our way to our eternal home? Shall we so live, so act, as to make fruitful the grace in our souls? Shall we take the affairs of everyday life and use them as means to reach our destiny? Hope governing all, hope strengthening all, eternal life ever our end? Let us "look not at the things which are seen, but at the things which are not seen. For the things which are seen, are temporal; but the things which are not seen, are eternal" (2 Cor. 4:18). Then to do all to please God will be a real joy; nothing will be too hard to do, nothing too easy to offer; obedience, mortifications imposed or self-inflicted, charity, humility, prayer, avoidance of sin and imperfection will have a new meaning, for they gain that welcome reward: "Come, ye blessed of my Father ... [into] the kingdom prepared for you" (Matt. 25:34). And we have reached home, are at home with God.

Chapter 17

∞

Charity

We should love God. As a matter of fact, we all want to love Him. We know that He has been good to us. We remember that He died for us. We appreciate the gift of faith and the call to follow that faith. We see that health, success in studies, and spiritual favors are graces from God. We understand that whatever we have, we have received from Him; that whatever we have accomplished, He gave the increase. We should love God. And our hearts cry out that we wish to love Him as much as we can, as much as we ought.

We should love God. In truth we want to love Him, and for that reason, are sorry that we have offended Him. Our sins are before us. Our sense of sin is more keen, deeper than it has ever been. We are sorry; we are resolved to do better; we want God to know that. We are anxious to make reparation in the best possible way. We want to love God as much as we can, as much as we ought. We desire to make our sorrow deepen our love.

We should love God. Our hearts cry out that we want to love Him. We are determined, with the help of grace, to lose even life itself rather than offend Him by mortal sin.

Rooting Out Hidden Faults

We ask for the grace to love Thee, Lord, to such a
degree as to be ready to lose all, rather than offend
Thee by a venial sin. Above all, help us to prove our
love by the way we live our vocation, by our constant
and persevering effort to be perfect. We beg the
grace to love Thee by the fervor and attention of our
prayers, by our zealous practice of recollection, by our
wholehearted application and attention to studies, by
our practice of all virtues in recreation, especially those
of charity and meekness. Lord, we want to love Thee;
help us to be perfect, for true love is shown by the way
we think and speak and act. We understand that fidelity
to our duties is the best way of showing our love to
Thee.

We should love God for His own sake. We should love Him
because He is infinitely worthy of being loved. He is God. We
should love Him for that reason alone.

Hermits have loved God. Alone in the silence of the forest,
they have walked with God. They sought shelter in its quietness;
they found solitude; they communed with God and loved Him.
Being away from the busy and, for them, distracting things of the
world, they saw God in the creatures about them. Not that they
necessarily loved nature — the trees, and the sun, and the stars,
the handiwork of God — but they wanted to be alone, to live for
God. Being alone, they thought, and rightly so, that they would
and could serve God more faithfully, for there are saints who
were hermits. Their obedience was to things of Faith — God's
law as explained by the Church. Their humility was made deep
by their love for Him for whom they had left all. Their mortification was all that the hermitage lacked in the good things of life.

Their virtue was prayer in the presence of Him whom they were constantly serving. Living their love in such a way, think you they were happy? Intensely so. The joy of a good conscience was theirs; they were loving the Master in the way that they thought best—by faithful service.

There were others who sought to live their love of God in the quietness of the forest, but they had companions. They felt that they could serve God better by having the help of others. They formed a community, living under a common rule. Their love of God was in obedience to the rule. Moreover, they were not only working for their own holiness; they were also helping others to salvation and sanctity. The power of their example went far beyond the confines of the forest or the community, so that many came to live with them, or at least to seek that spiritual advice that would be a source of help and encouragement. Such persons, going back to the world, would actually preach what they had seen and heard. Many would be told how the communities in the desert were living the Faith.

Others serve God faithfully and thus show their love for Him. These cannot seek salvation or holiness in living alone, nor can they choose the life of a community. They really belong in the world. They have their duties to perform in the world, and they must not shirk them. They must live where their vocation calls them. Many saints have lived in the world. They sought their holiness in the ordinary affairs of life. They had work to do, and they did it well; they had prayers to say, and they said them well; they enjoyed the innocent pleasures allowed to those seeking higher things. They did not sigh and complain that the world in which duty made them stay was keeping them from becoming good and even saintly. They accepted the trials and difficulties such an obligation imposed and made it a means of serving God and thus proving their love for Him. In fact, such difficulties for them were things of joy, for they were doing all for God, knowing that to suffer for the Lord was to follow the Master truly.

There are many who have served and loved God perfectly in the world. They are in every walk of life. There is the saint of the countryside; there is the saint of the throne and the saint of the hovel. There are still more in the world who serve God and love Him, but not perfectly. They are faithful to what God has revealed; they are attentive to their duties as Catholics; they are concerned about living well; they are the many thousands of good fathers and mothers, good sisters and brothers. How zealous they are to be what conscience tells them to be! What effort they make to be fervent Catholics! How they do love the Church! How they love God, as shown by their faithfulness to duty!

Many have sought to love God in the practice of poverty, chastity, and obedience. Under the vows, they follow others to real goodness of life. They know that the more completely they follow the Master, the greater will be their joy. They may feel the yoke at times, but they realize that it is sweet and light; or if it is heavy, they are glad and rejoice that the Master would have it so. They understand that to love God is to serve Him faithfully; they know that the more faithfully they serve Him, the greater will be their love for Him.

We who are following a vocation should try to acquire a strong, zealous, flaming love of God by endeavoring to live our vocation in a constantly more perfect way, by asking God to give us the grace to love Him, by begging Him to make us love Him, by repeatedly making acts of love, by doing His will as perfectly as we can. We should conform our wills to His. We should try to think as He thinks, to act as He acts, to speak as He speaks. We can practice that conformity by seeing His will in everything.

Those who love God seek to make others love Him. There are many who have the true Faith who do not love God as they should. There are many not of the Faith who do not love Him. Vocations are needed. Look at the necessities of the Church: fallen-away Catholics should he brought back; ordinary good Catholics should be made better; those close to holiness should be made holier. Not only should we do all in our power to awaken vocations, but we should also do all that we can to encourage perseverance in vocation. God wants all men to love and serve Him. Could we do more to bring God's wish about? Zeal for souls is a great way of showing our love for God.

Let us, then, love God and serve Him, because He has been good to us, because we have offended Him, because we should love Him, for He is God. Let us love God and serve Him; by the way we live our vocation in the ordinary affairs of daily life, by our zeal in striving for perfection, and by our ardor in helping others to holiness and eternal life.

Charity toward Self

We should love ourselves in the right way. This is not that self-love that is a false love of self. We should take reasonable care of health and physical fitness, thereby avoiding too much concern about them. Aches and pains and even severe suffering are to be patiently and silently borne. Thinking about them increases the selfish tendency to speak about them. If we are well, let us thank God; if we are ill, let us willingly suffer and thereby grow in virtue. In fact, if we can, we should allow no external sign to show that we are suffering. We should accept God's providential care, knowing and believing that all things tend to holiness and salvation, if we will only view matters with eyes that look to the world to come.

Rooting Out Hidden Faults

We should love ourselves in the right way in regard to our work. What obedience places upon us, we should accept cheerfully. In truth, any burden is a joy when we labor for the Lord. If strength is needed for our work, we give what we have, knowing that that is all that is expected. If aptitude is required, we offer whatever fitness we have, understanding that no more is asked. If the work is tedious or not to our liking, we should hold fast to our spirit of obedience. So many are prone to self-love where there is a question of manual labor. Are we really working for God? We should keep that thought in mind, remembering that we are trying to please Him.

We should love ourselves in the right way in regard to studies. Let us realize that we study not merely for the development of the mind. Intellectual accomplishments should be spiritual, training character, giving strength to the soul, helping us on the road to eternal life. Yet self-love often enters into study. Application and silence and attention are hard; perseverance is still harder; faithful seeking after learning and scholarship is most difficult. Self-love is self-pity, refusing to impose burdens on self, anxious to take things easy, being satisfied with more or less success; and if there is failure, self-love is ready to place the blame on others by declaring that lack of zeal was not wanting, nor lack of ability, and so there is censure, faultfinding criticism, misjudgment, false comparison. If we love self in the right way, we shall serve God by working for Him. We should give our best efforts, knowing that God will be satisfied.

We should love ourselves in the right way in regard to spiritual affairs. Holiness is a personal, individual concern. So is salvation. No matter what the standard of others is, the only important consideration for me is: What is my standard? What is my motive of conduct? For whom am I working? Am I serving self? Then

I love self. Am I serving God? Then I love God. Certainly our resolution should be to love God and to serve Him more and more faithfully.

True spiritual progress demands that each one forget self. Virtue is forgetfulness of self. Obedience means giving up one's will; mortification is self-denial; humility is giving God credit for what we do; prayerfulness is acknowledging our dependence on God; charity is love of God and neighbor; avoidance of sin and imperfection is a refusal to allow self undue liberty. The practice of any virtue necessitates some suppression of self. Hence, spiritual progress demands that we conform our will to God's will. Perfection is the fulfillment of God's will.

If we love ourselves in the right way, we shall use all things to serve God and to love Him. Service increases love, and love increases service.

Love of Neighbor

We should love our neighbor. Jesus, our Model, has given us the example; the saints followed it; so should we. "I have called you friends," Jesus says (John 15:15). He loved everybody, even the sinner, though He hated sin. Rich and poor, good and bad, the needy and the afflicted all received from the abundance of His heart. He died for all. "Greater love than this no man hath, that a man lay down His life for his friends" (John 15:13).

We should love our neighbor. Who is my neighbor? There is a love that is due the members of our own family. There is a love that is owed to relatives, those who have been good to us, our friends, those who have authority over us, those who oppose us, those who do not love us. We need not love these with an equal love. Love has degrees of intensity. In other words, we must love all, though not in the same degree. Now, as we show our love of God by serving Him, so we manifest our love of neighbor by giving respect and, where it is due, obedience. "All things whatsoever you would that men should do unto you, do you also to them" (see Matt. 7:12).

Love of neighbor is a command. "These things I command you, that you love one another" (John 15:17). More than that, "by this all men know that you are my disciples, if you have love one for another" (see John 13:35). "If therefore thou offer thy gift at the altar, and there thou remember that thy brother hath any thing against thee, leave there thy offering before the altar, and go first to be reconciled to thy brother: and then coming thou shalt offer thy gift" (Matt. 5:23–24). Love of neighbor is a command, a sign of our following the Master, a necessity if we are to be friends of God.

In what does our love of neighbor consist? Certainly not in jealousy, envy, rash judgment, criticism; nor in seeing faults; nor in lack of patience and meekness. Perhaps more than anything else, it does not consist in an unbridled tongue. How inconsiderate the tongue can be, how ready to utter unkind, uncharitable, angry, critical words! How prone to be malicious, revealing the true or starting the false, and thereby sending forth a poison that enters into the hearts of others, stirring up dislike and enmity! "If any man offend not in word, the same is a perfect man"; "And if any man think himself to be religious, not bridling his tongue, but deceiving his own heart, this man's religion is vain" (Jas. 3:2; 1:26).

Love of neighbor thrives on kindliness, on a spirit that is considerate in thought, word, and deed; a spirit that means peace with all, friendliness with all, love for all; a spirit that is generous in sympathy, rich with meekness, deep with consideration for the happiness of others. We may not, as a matter of fact, have much opportunity to practice the corporal works of mercy: feeding the hungry, giving drink to the thirsty, clothing the naked, giving hospitality to strangers, visiting the sick, redeeming captives, and burying the dead. Nevertheless, there is much that each one of us can do in carrying out the spiritual works of mercy: we can correct sinners, we can teach the ignorant, we can counsel the doubting, we can console the sorrowful and the afflicted, we can bear injuries patiently, and we can pray for the salvation of others.

Love of neighbor demands fraternal correction. Prudence, kindliness, meekness, and zeal for souls should prompt us to help others by correcting them. We should be anxious to see others physically fit; we should be concerned about seeing them take proper care of the work assigned them and still more concerned about their success in studies; above all, we should be eager to see their spiritual successes. Prudent and kind and meek corrections can help. Cowards refuse to accept this duty; the charitable follow it. How do you stand? What is your state of mind? Would you willingly allow another to be an influence for evil to himself and to his associates? Would you stand by and watch how souls are deliberately ruined? If you have the right state of mind, if you love your neighbor, and as yet do not understand how to offer advice by way of correction, if you do not know how to draw another from erring, speak to your superior, or confessor, or spiritual director, for no general rule can be proposed that would cover every case. Learn how to correct by following the advice of another. Be on fire with zeal for God, for the Church — love your neighbor.

Now, there is no surer way of loving our neighbor than by correcting our own faults. Some have much to do in this regard; others not so much; but all of us have something. The concern we have in keeping ourselves in subjection will show itself in charity. The fewer faults we are guilty of, the less ready shall we be to fall into faults against charity; the more faults we have, the easier will be our fall. Charity is the sign of one's standard, of one's goodness, of one's perfection. Yet there are those who seemingly have a high spiritual standard but are woefully wanting in charity. As a matter of fact, they are no better than their charity.

There is no better way of loving our neighbor than by giving a good example. We give a good example by not giving a bad example. Too much emphasis cannot be placed on this. The spirit of a house or any group of associates depends on good example. If we fulfill our duties, we help others to fulfill theirs. We certainly do influence others or at least someone. Consequently, we owe even that one an example that is good. If I keep the rules, I help someone else to do the same; if I am meek, I aid another to be meek; any virtue that is practiced cannot help but be an influence for good. Do all of us realize our obligation? Should we not be happy in thinking that we are aiding others to do what is right? Let us try to be sources of edification.

It stands to reason that if we love God in the right way, we shall love ourselves in the right way, and we shall love our neighbor in the right way. Let one of these loves be wrong, and there will be something wanting in the other two. Now is the time to straighten out anything that may be wrong. Now is the time to follow the full meaning of the commandment: "Thou shalt love the Lord thy God with thy whole heart, and with thy whole soul, and with thy whole mind. This is the greatest and the first commandment. And the second is like to this: Thou shalt love thy neighbour as thyself" (Matt. 22:37–39).

Chapter 18

∞

Prudence

Prudence is a moral virtue that enables us to decide what is right and proper to do in particular cases. It deliberates on the way to render actions good; it judges whether such and such a way is suitable as well as good; it commands the will to follow the judgment.

Our Faith should help us to be prudent. The teachings of the Church, sermons, conferences, spiritual reading, and spiritual advice are the unfolding of that Faith, guiding us aright by giving us correct principles of conduct. To understand such principles, to remember them, and effectively to follow them in practice is to keep from error.

There is no more ready way of being imprudent than by refusing to take advice. Are we prepared to listen to it, to accept it gladly? Certainly we can lose nothing by listening to it, weighing it against our own views or convictions, and determining whether or not to follow it. Moreover, we should remember that criticism is very often nothing more than advice. Simply to pass by such unfavorable comment, ignoring it or giving it no true consideration or deliberation, is not to be reasonable. A fool could warn us against folly; a sinner against sin; a worldling against the deceits of the world; how much more precious is the criticism of a friend or even one not so friendly. Prudence analyzes criticism, even when it is personal, to judge whether there is any basis for it. If it is true wholly or in part, then good use is made of it; if it is not true, then a guard is placed to prevent it from becoming true. After all, criticism is nothing more than fraternal correction. Yet how prone we are not to want to hear it, not to give it due attention, not to use it in a helpful way.

More than likely, we are ready to accept advice from one who freely offers it. However, there is a further step: Do we ask for advice? Mistakes will be avoided and greater things will be accomplished thereby. Experience is a teacher. Are we among those who trust in it, when it comes from one who is capable and backed by authority? If it is reasonable and helpful to listen to advice, is it not also reasonable and helpful to seek it? Much imprudence would be avoided if we sought counsel, getting the views and convictions of others.

How quickly imprudence can creep into ordinary affairs of everyday life. The care of the body should be reasonable; yet too much concern or too little can be bad. We should guard health, of course, but not beyond the norm of reason. Too much anxiety about personal appearance is really worse than too little; foppishness, fastidiousness in dress, is more to be condemned than that which is poor. Neglect of the rules of etiquette is no more to be tolerated than affected manners. External manners should be a sign of inward culture; a gentleman is a gentleman every day of the week. Now, prudence would so regulate these ordinary concerns that excess and defect are avoided. Better far if care of health, concern for personal appearance, and observance of all the ordinary rules of etiquette were spiritual and not merely natural. The body is the temple of the Holy Ghost; we are following a vocation. We should keep both these ideas in mind, seeking a culture that is becoming to followers of the Master.

By taking and receiving advice, we will be helped in avoiding imprudence in regard to our mental development. A right state of mind is necessary concerning education, which should not be mere mental training. A brilliant mind is not everything; moral success is vastly more important. To neglect the soul for the mind would be unwise, unreasonable, and contrary to the true end of life — holiness and salvation. Learning, scholarship, and culture should be regulated by principles of conduct. The true Faith, God revealing and the Church teaching, is the rule that will guide us aright.

There are too many cases of education being sought at the expense of religion. Some spend their powers in intellectual pursuits to the neglect of the soul. They may gain glory and fame, but will they save their souls? What does it profit a man if his soul be lost? In our day, not only is there a neglect of religion in state education, but there are also insidious, open, and even malicious attacks upon it. How imprudent to allow oneself to be misled by false leaders! How imprudent to accept mental development at such a cost! How imprudent to gain the world and lose one's soul!

Though it may be perfectly true that we have the right attitude toward education, have we, perhaps, been imprudent in study? Prudence forbids excess as well as defect. Are our studies a part of our spiritual life? Does study occupy so much time as to mean a neglect of spiritual duties? On the other hand, do we persevere with steady application and attention and willingness to learn? Do we plan our work, giving it wholehearted effort, so as to get not only the required but also the most fruitful result? Do we aim to develop a memory that is truly retentive, an understanding that is more and more capable, an imagination that is sensitive, a power of reasoning that is governed by logical principles, a will that is firm in seeking right and avoiding wrong? What use have we made of our opportunities to advance mentally?

Have we had an imprudent state of mind concerning those who teach us? Students are prone to criticize, to ridicule, to misjudge, to accuse of unfairness. Concern for success, selfish interests, wrong comparisons, a false sense of humor, and even lack of study are the reasons. Now, as a matter of fact, too much emphasis has been placed on the ability of the teacher. No one denies that a scholarly and inspirational teacher is a great help to the student, but admitting that the teacher is neither scholarly nor inspiring, should not the prudent and therefore proper state of mind suggest that each and every one try to get as much as he can from every study? Would not prudence demand, if our studies are to be spiritual, if we are doing all for God, that we bring our talents to bear on each study and carry away all that we can? Would not prudence forbid disrespect, faultfinding, ridicule, a spirit of opposition? Would not prudence require that we check up on our study standard by asking advice?

We should accept advice about spiritual affairs, and ask for it. Our knowledge of the Faith should increase, bringing new understanding. Progress in virtue should be made; wrong should be more easily avoided. There is so much that we can learn about the ordinary affairs of daily spiritual life. Increased knowledge is helpful to fervent practice. It is reasonable to suppose that advice coming from one who is competent and fit will be of assistance. Difficulties will be more readily met.

Let us go through the prayers of the day.

Are our meditations fruitful?

Are our assistance at Mass, reception of Communion,
    and thanksgiving fervent?

Is the Particular Examen a means of progress?

Are our prayers fervent and attentive?

Are they said with humble and persevering confidence?

Have we any difficulty about prompt, cheerful, entire,
supernatural obedience?

Do we know enough about practicing mortification
of the mind and the senses?

Do we understand the virtue of humility?

Do we realize what is meant by love of God and neighbor?

Is there any virtue that we find hard to practice? Any
temptation that worries us?

Could we not learn more about faithfully practicing
our daily duties?

Have we sought advice and followed it?

Prudence demands that we take the right attitude toward our spiritual duties. Holiness has suffered from imprudence. There was a day when daily or even frequent Communion was considered a spiritual food for saints only. Piety has been ridiculed; so has rule keeping; so have obedience and humility and mortification and meekness. Scoffers have attacked virtue in general, claiming that it is a sign of weakness, not of strength. They foolishly assert that courage is needed to do wrong. Seemingly those who do not care to be good, who do not care to do the right thing, are reckless enough to indulge in the meanest and lowest type of criticism — ridicule of those who are conscientiously following the Master.

Holiness is not oddity. Yet sometimes those who seek godliness allow peculiarities to creep in. It is urged that certain saints were odd. Yet it should be remembered that saints are saints in spite of such peculiarities. The saints were human and normal; oddity is not canonized, though pious writers have at times made much of a peculiarity. Holiness is the sum total of all virtue. Any defect detracts. A faithful and impartial history of any saint will reveal the qualities that made him holy.

Holiness has suffered from imprudent thinking and practice. Again, it is well to say that sanctity is made up of many qualities. Goodness is not piety alone; goodness is not rule keeping alone; holiness is not humility alone. A saint who is noted for obedience had other virtues; a saint noted for love of God, or humility, or meekness had other virtues. Nevertheless there are many who do not see that holiness is doing ordinary things well. Apparently they do not understand that goodness embraces prayer and study, work and play. Prudence keeps straight the state of mind in regard to these daily obligations. Prudence keeps right the state of mind regarding holiness.

Therefore, it behooves those who are endeavoring to be holy not to be given to imprudence. Too often a person with a reputation for holiness has some glaring weakness. This one is considered almost a saint, but he is decidedly slovenly; another is cranky and uncharitable; a third is too serious and condemns reasonable gaiety; a fourth is very pious and prays much, yet his judgment is bad; a fifth keeps the rules perfectly, though he has a ready tongue for the faults of others. Still others considered holy are sarcastic, given to dishonesty in games, have a reputation for untruthfulness, are envious, or have a false sense of humor. Now, no one is any better than his worst fault. While one outstanding quality does not make a person holy, one predominating fault can keep one from being even good. True, anyone may fall into faults, but holiness is not had by one committing chronic — that is, continued — faults of the same kind. Consequently, to seek holiness is to correct any predominating fault. Wrongdoing should not become a habit.

There are those who fall into imprudent practices. They make innumerable Signs of the Cross; they moan, or sigh, or weep; they become sentimentally pious; they multiply prayers; they have so many devotions that they cannot pray well; they stay at prayer to the neglect of duty; they complain that common exercises take them away from their private prayers. Such persons would be helped by prudent advice.

Are we prudent? Have we the right state of mind concerning prayer and study and work and play? Have we tried to keep in mind the spirit of things and not the mere letter? Have we taken advice, sought it and followed it?[7]

[7] We preferred to treat some questions under prudence that more properly could have been treated under temperance.

Chapter 19

∞

Justice

Justice is a moral virtue that disposes the will to give everyone his due. "Render to Caesar the things that are Caesar's; and to God, the things that are God's" (see Matt. 22:21).

"Render to God the things that are God's." Adore Him, praise Him, give Him the honor and reverence that are due to Him. Would that our joy and promptitude, our desires and aspirations, our affections were so true of our service of God that temporal concerns, pleasure, lack of spiritual delight could not lessen our fervor. Would that our reparation for past wrong was so heartfelt that we would not draw away from His service! Would that our gratitude, our obedience, our reverence, our persevering faithfulness to Him were expressed in daily goodness of life!

Now, is it not true that, in rendering our dues to God, we are disrespectful? Is there not some irreverence in the way we make the Sign of the Cross, in the way we genuflect and kneel? Are we not somewhat unmindful of the rubrics? Do not our prayers lack something? We know that the absence of spiritual delight and the presence of aridities make praying hard; yet would not the overcoming of that difficulty raise the standard of prayer simply because of the required effort? Faithfulness to prayer is a duty even when fervor is lacking. So also for attention. We understand that attention can be paid to the words, or to the meaning of the words, or to God. Distractions will come, to be sure, but need we irreverently give way to them? Should not our purpose be to acquire such control of our minds that our prayers will always rise from our hearts: with confidence, in humility, perseveringly? Why speak to God irreverently? Why be discourteous when we talk to Him?

"Render to Caesar the things that are Caesar's." Authority is sacred; it comes from God. Yet in our day conscientious respect for law is lacking; in fact, disrespect for law is rampant. People seem to think that there is a moral responsibility on the governing or the governed. There is a tendency to tear down authority. We are required to be obedient, law-abiding citizens. Patriotism is not mere emotional display or talk; it is a sincere love of country and respect for its laws and rules. Faithfulness to God should help us to be true to the state and nation. Faithfulness to God is faithfulness to Caesar.

We should love, respect, and obey our parents and their representatives. Too often those subject to obedience forget that those in authority are bound in conscience to exercise their duties. If love and respect are wanting, there arises dislike with its fruitful breed: criticism, faultfinding, perhaps even ridicule. Then what becomes of obedience? It ceases to be prompt; it certainly is not cheerful; it surely is not wholehearted; and it is not for God. Would that all our obedience were to the Lord!

We should respect the rights of our neighbor. The reputation of each one is to be held sacred. Charity to all is a duty; consideration for everyone is an obligation. All in all to all—friends with everybody, but not too friendly with anyone. Have we failed to respect the rights of our neighbor by gossiping? Have we been discourteous, unkind, and inconsiderate? If we have gossiped about our neighbors, we have likely criticized them, revealing their faults, and perhaps lied about them or held grudges against them. If we have kept true to charity, then we think of the happiness of others and particularly of those with whom we associate. Good example follows charity; bad example goes with uncharitableness.

Our state of life demands rules. Without such guides there would be chaos. What is our attitude toward them? They can be deemed trivial, unimportant, and perhaps even unnecessary. However, they regulate liberty for the sake of the common good; they are based on experience; they have the approval of authority; they are a means to holiness. To look upon them as ways to develop character is to have the proper state of mind. To follow them consciously is to serve God better.

Justice requires that we be honest and truthful. Yet some seem little concerned about trivial bits of dishonesty and untruthfulness. They use both as means to get out of difficulties. They overlook fair play and the rules of sportsmanship; promises are readily made and easily forgotten or broken; lies are used in self-defense or for fun; dishonest methods are used to win. What about one's reputation? What about bad example? What about following the Master?

Not much of an examination of conscience should be necessary to determine just how we are rendering our duties to God, to Caesar, and to our neighbor. Is there need of resolutions? Where we have failed in our duties, we should make reparation. Certainly we have offended God. Satisfaction must be made by doing penance, through prayers, by abstinence and fast, by saying the penance imposed by our confessor, and by penances we impose on ourselves. However, no one fails to remember that satisfaction must be made to God; yet we do forget that, when we have injured our neighbor, reparation must also be made. Restitution is not the only thing required by justice. If we have injured another's reputation, detracted or slandered that other, given bad example, been uncharitable, been a source of unhappiness or hurt another in any way, we must repair the damage. Have we done so, making as full a reparation as possible?

Chapter 20

∞

Fortitude

Fortitude is a moral virtue that, for the purpose of doing good, inspires us to great and difficult works, or enables us to suffer grave evils, even death itself.

The hero, having strength of will and purpose, is held in admiration; the coward, having weakness of will and purpose, is condemned. Yet men have commonly called heroic that which demands physical prowess, physical courage. Those noted for mental achievements have not been termed heroic, though their genius is recognized. Still, one who stands for principle, who remains true to it, who resolutely follows it, is a hero.

Now, heroism is not within marked limits. Just where it begins and ends and where folly enters cannot be accurately determined. The quality of courage should not lead to a false self-confidence, which ordinarily is expressed in egotism, in a domineering spirit, in unnecessary risks. Self-reliance should not be willful neglect of prudent safeguards. Self-determination should not be deliberate refusal to accept advice. Overconfidence is as bad as timidity. Both are abnormal and need to be made sane and reasonable. Foolishly to attempt what is beyond one's powers is to court disaster; not to try what one could reasonably do is to accept failure.

Rooting Out Hidden Faults

Moral courage, that is, fortitude, is often lacking in those who have physical and mental strength as well as in those who have not. Human respect and timidity enter into what they do or avoid. They see a bad example and follow it; they observe others doing wrong, and they have not the courage to do right; they are afraid of the opinion of others; they listen to things that they disapprove of; they keep silent when they should speak. They become followers instead of leaders.

Fortitude, greatness of soul, should incline us to heroic acts of every kind of virtue. We do not allow ourselves to be presumptuous, that is, attempt what is not prudent. Nor do we permit ourselves to be ambitious, that is, strive for power for its own sake. Nor do we suffer vainglory to be the motive of conduct. Nor should we allow weakness of character or false confidence to rule us. We aim at perfection of virtue, though not all virtues at once. We seek holiness, though the approach is slow and hard and little by little.

Have we worked in a truly heroic way? Most of us will not face grave dangers or death by martyrdom. Still, there is heroism in being faithful to ordinary duties. It is no easy matter to be perfect from day to day. It is hard to give up one's will completely, to be an exemplar of self-denial, to be prayerful, to be sincerely humble, to keep rules perfectly, to avoid sin and imperfection perseveringly, to love God with our whole heart and our neighbor as ourselves. As a matter of fact, there may not be perfection in every detail, but the great thing to be accomplished is kept in mind and sought for constantly. There is an effort to bring self into subjection. An absolute victory over self is heroism.

Temptation, of course, will try to prevent perseverance. If it cannot stop us from starting, it will attempt to keep us from continuing. Now, perseverance is nothing less than forgetfulness of self. What is sought is kept in mind and not the personal effort required to reach it. The burden and heat are borne for the good cause that is sought. Our Lord thought of the work to be accomplished. The apostles were ready to be sacrificed because of the good tidings that they were bringing to others for the sake of the Master. St. Paul expressed this thought most adequately when he said that he was willing to be anathema if it would serve the glory of God (see Rom. 9:3). That was complete forgetfulness of self. On the contrary, we are inclined to put much on personal whim and fancy and difficulty. Seemingly, we hate to work hard to acquire things, even those of value. If perseverance were looked on with eyes of faith — an opportunity to serve God, a chance to help others, a means of acquiring learning and holiness — then we would face resolutely the mountaintops and struggle along securely and slowly to reach them, knowing that our trust is not in self alone but in God. Moreover, if we look at perseverance as something that applies to the very action that we are performing, and not as to some distant thing, we will face the future confidently, trusting to God.

There will be temptations to waver. We have not developed perfect habits of constancy. Steadiness of purpose has to be acquired. All of us are somewhat weak and somewhat changeable. If we fall, if we break our resolutions, should we not rise promptly, take heart again, and follow through to the journey's end?

In other words, there will be difficulties. So many take the wrong view of them. Temptations worry them; trials cause loss of peace of mind, bringing discontent and even discouragement; faithfulness to daily duties seem hard, especially when there is lack of spiritual delight. A sane and spiritual idea of difficulties should be had. They prove us; they test us; they give us an opportunity to work harder for God. They do not mean that there is something wrong with us or our spiritual life; when overcome, they do declare that we are on the right road spiritually. To let them conquer us is to go along with the current, following the line of least resistance, and that leads to nothing great. Life is a warfare. Cowards refuse to fight or offer feeble opposition. The courageous glory in the chance to prove their mettle to God. There is joy in victory that is fought for. The strong of heart do not give up.

Let our trust and our strength be in God. "The Lord is my protector; of whom shall I be afraid?" (see Ps. 26:1 [27:1]). Let us be constant in following good. Let us perseveringly overcome difficulties. Let us seek perfection in our ordinary affairs. Let us strive unceasingly to love God, for then we shall do great things for Him.

Chapter 21

∞

Temperance

Temperance is a moral virtue that enables us to use, according to right reason, things that are agreeable to the senses. "Continence checks movements of the will goaded on by the assault of passion; meekness, to which clemency is allied, restrains motions of anger tending to revenge; modesty regulates external motions and words, and care, also of the body and all external pomp; studiousness governs eagerness for knowledge; humility represses the desire of excellence; reserve tempers ludicrous and jocose movements." Temperance in regard to eating and drinking has been discussed in the chapter on gluttony; temperance concerning meekness has been treated under anger; study under sloth and pride; continence under lust; humility under pride.

Temperance would have us keep in mind that we are developing not merely natural, but spiritual character. We are seeking to make principle the right motive, the influence of what we do, so that we may serve God better and help others to do the same. We are preparing for another world. There should be moderation in everything, so that we may reach our destined end. The perfect person is well-regulated, erring neither from excess nor defect.

Rooting Out Hidden Faults

Temperance demands modesty. Exterior modesty should be a sign of interior modesty. Becoming conduct should reveal inward culture. Religious reserve should not be a veneer, a cloak, a shield, but something based on qualities of soul. Normal good taste and spiritual training are helps to modesty. Assuredly there is something lacking in the person who is singular in walk, in sitting or kneeling positions. Certainly fastidiousness is no more to be tolerated than boorishness. There is always the question of good example in regard to these.

There is a reserve proper to recreation that condemns boisterousness, giddiness, frivolity, rowdy conduct. There is the modesty of good sportsmanship required of those who win as well as those who lose. There is a dignified interest in sports. There is a sense of good taste and refinement in fun that is had by those who remember the presence of our Lord. There is a proper view of amusements, which often are lawful, but not expedient. All in all, reserve is nothing more than knowing what is right and doing it; moderation is keeping in control unruly passions and senses; culture is consideration for others. Temperance is the keeping of a reasonable balance.

To have moderation of study is to be reasonable about it. An inordinate desire of knowledge is usually accompanied by neglect of other duties; an inordinate zeal in seeking knowledge is certainly a neglect of other obligations; a lazy attitude in studies is assuredly a guilty neglect. Our duty is to fit ourselves for our state of life. We are held to know what is proper to it and what will help us to take care of it most efficiently. Our obligation is clear. Throughout life we should be students, studiously seeking to develop ourselves so as to meet fully our mental and spiritual duties.

We are teaching others. That means we are helping them to develop spiritual character. Good example is necessary. Fair play, humility, and charity should be practiced by every teacher; so should truthfulness. Pupils are followers; they thrive on judicious authority; they are easily influenced. Leadership that inspires, that creates a spirit and love of study, that builds strong wills for good are qualities that bearers of truth should have. Mental and spiritual progress on the part of teachers will most certainly mean mental and spiritual progress on the part of students.

Moderation in things demands rules: common and personal ones. The former are made by those in authority; the latter by the individual. A well-regulated habit of life is a decided advantage, if there are reasonable exceptions. No one should be a slave to method. There is a time for everything, and usually there is time for everything, if a plan of action is followed. Promptness and faithfulness to a daily schedule must have fruitful results: much will be done, and in a better way, and eventually there will be ample opportunity to take up some special interest of prayer, or study, or recreation.

One great help to orderly living is a spirit of silence. Someone has said that a conversationalist is one who knows how to listen. Talkativeness is not an expression of thought, for thought requires reflection. Very often the shallow, personal, selfish, and false are the subjects of those who talk much; or there is a descent to the critical and gossipy. Now, who is there that has not been intemperate in speech? Who is there who has not been immoderate and angry in argument, imprudent in statement, unreserved in tone? Who is there that has not offended by tongue? Only the perfect man. The calm, meek, deliberate thinker has ordinarily trained himself by silence to converse well. Certainly silence is an aid to fidelity in study and prayer.

Who has a standard that is singularly high? The temperate person. Who is meek and clement? The temperate person. Who has refined manners? The temperate person. Who has the right point of view of games, of work, of studies, of spiritual duties? The temperate person. Who has a character that is affable, agreeable, friendly, lovable? Who has something of that gentleness of soul, that heart of virtue, that perfection so characteristic of our Lord? The temperate person. Become perfect by being temperate in all things.

Sophia Institute

Sophia Institute is a nonprofit institution that seeks to nurture the spiritual, moral, and cultural life of souls and to spread the gospel of Christ in conformity with the authentic teachings of the Roman Catholic Church.

Sophia Institute Press fulfills this mission by offering translations, reprints, and new publications that afford readers a rich source of the enduring wisdom of mankind.

Sophia Institute also operates the popular online resource CatholicExchange.com. *Catholic Exchange* provides world news from a Catholic perspective as well as daily devotionals and articles that will help readers to grow in holiness and live a life consistent with the teachings of the Church.

In 2013, Sophia Institute launched Sophia Institute for Teachers to renew and rebuild Catholic culture through service to Catholic education. With the goal of nurturing the spiritual, moral, and cultural life of souls, and an abiding respect for the role and work of teachers, we strive to provide materials and programs that are at once enlightening to the mind and ennobling to the heart; faithful and complete, as well as useful and practical.

Sophia Institute gratefully recognizes the Solidarity Association for preserving and encouraging the growth of our apostolate over the course of many years. Without their generous and timely support, this book would not be in your hands.

www.SophiaInstitute.com
www.CatholicExchange.com
www.SophiaInstituteforTeachers.org

Sophia Institute Press® is a registered trademark of Sophia Institute.
Sophia Institute is a tax-exempt institution as defined by the
Internal Revenue Code, Section 501(c)(3). Tax ID 22-2548708.